Books by Richard B. Lyttle

PEOPLE OF THE DAWN
Early Man in the Americas

WAVES ACROSS THE PAST
Adventures in Underwater Archaeology

THE GAMES THEY PLAYED
Sports in History

THE GOLDEN PATH
The Lure of Gold Through History

LAND BEYOND THE RIVER
Europe in the Age of Migration

IL DUCE
The Rise & Fall of Benito Mussolini

IL DUCE

The Rise & Fall of Benito Mussolini

IL DUCE

ATHENEUM · NEW YORK · 1987

The Rise & Fall of

Benito Mussolini

by Richard B. Lyttle

Atheneum
Macmillan Publishing Company
866 Third Avenue, New York, NY 10022
Collier Macmillan Canada, Inc.

Type set by Haddon Craftsmen, Allentown, Pennsylvania
Printed and bound by Fairfield Graphics, Fairfield, Pennsylvania
Designed by Mary Ahern
First Edition

10   9   8   7   6   5   4   3   2   1

Library of Congress Cataloging-in-Publication Data

Lyttle, Richard B.
Il duce: the rise and fall of Benito Mussolini.

Bibliography: p. 206
Includes index.
1. Mussolini, Benito, 1883–1945. 2. Italy—Politics and
government—1914–1945. 3. Fascism—Italy—History—20th
century. 4. Heads of state—Italy—Biography. I. Title.
DG575.M8L98   1987   945.091'092'4 [B]   86-28851
ISBN 0-689-31213-X

This book is for
KEENE HALDEMAN

CONTENTS

Il Duce

The Rise & Fall of Benito Mussolini

1

Early Years

HE WAS BORN between two and three on the afternoon of July 29, 1883, in Varano di Costa, a small, poor Italian village forty-five miles east of Bologna. His mother, Rosa Maltoni Mussolini, twenty-five, was an elementary grade school teacher. His father, Alessandro Gaspare Mussolini, twenty-eight, was a blacksmith who had made the sturdy iron bed in which the couple's first child was born.

Rosa, a proud Catholic, insisted on an early baptism for the baby. Alessandro named the child, and to no one's surprise, he chose revolutionary names. The boy was christened Benito Amilcare Andrea Mussolini. Benito was for Benito Juarez, the hero of Mexican independence, who gave his country a liberal and progressive government. Amilcare and Andrea were for two of Italy's revolutionary Socialists—Amilcare Cipriani and Andrea Costa.

Young Benito's father was himself proud to be a revolutionary Socialist. Although he had never been to school, he could read and write and had taught himself a technical trade that required a good deal of mathematical knowledge. Alessandro Mussolini was best known, however, as a persuasive speaker and writer. At Socialist party meetings he attacked the government, the king, and all forms of organized religion. His revolutionary articles appeared regularly in Socialist journals.

Alessandro headed the local branch of the Socialist party, and he headed the list of troublemakers watched by the police. He had served six months in jail for revolutionary activities and had remained under police surveillance.

As a result, young Benito grew up in a revolutionary climate. Later in life he recalled the hours he had spent sitting on the floor of his father's shop listening to party leaders plan the overthrow of Italy's ruling class.

Hidden in a chest in the shop basement was the red flag of revolution. It was brought out on May Day to be touched and admired. The rest of the year it remained hidden. Benito's father and his friends dreamed of the day when red banners would wave from every flagstaff in Italy.

Alessandro's revolutionary ideas reflected the general discontent of Italy's lower class. The country was poor. Some areas lacked rudimentary sanitation. Many regions were without schools. Rail and river transportation was limited. Farming was the major industry, but farming methods were primitive, and it was difficult to get crops to market.

The Italian government was ineffective. Taxes, oppressive in some regions, were not collected in others. The legal system was known more for its delays and corruption than for its justice. Because of the high level of illiteracy, little more than 20 percent of the population was qualified to vote.

Adding to Italy's problems was the highest birth rate in Europe. In the twenty years prior to Benito's birth the country's population had risen by 13 percent to a total of 29.5 million people. Housing, education, and employment had not kept up with the growth.

Many begged or turned to crime. Highway robbers made travel dangerous. During this era many young people left Italy to find work in other countries, usually as untrained laborers. Those who stayed home sometimes plotted revolution.

Benito heard some of his father's friends argue that the unification of Italy in 1861 had been a mistake. It would be better to return to preunification days, when each province was ruled as a separate kingdom. True, some rulers had been tyrants, but most had tried to keep their people happy and well fed.

Although others said unification was necessary for Italy's destiny as a civilized nation, all agreed that unification had seriously divided the country, setting the Church and the government against each other.

When the new parliamentary government was formed it claimed the responsibility for education, appointments of clergymen, administration of parishes, and the ownership of vast tracts of land that once were controlled by the Church. Contending that the government was taking authority that was theirs by tradition, leaders of the Church from the pope on down refused to recognize the new government. As the dispute grew hot, the Church banned Catholics from holding government office or even voting. The ban was not strictly enforced or observed; but just the same, it did keep some good people from entering government service at a time when good people were desperately needed.

The dispute divided all citizens into two camps: the Blacks who supported the Church, and the Whites who supported the government.

Largely because of the Church's ban on politics, Italy's Senate and Chamber of Deputies were made up of wealthy aristocrats who knew little about the country's problems or how to deal with them.

Most of Italy's poorest provinces, primarily those south of Rome, were not even represented in Parliament. Revolts in the south in 1877 and again in 1879 had been suppressed with bloodshed and without reforms. More violence was sure to come.

Changes, revolutionary changes, seemed the only cure for Italy's problems. Young Benito grew up with the conviction that change must come.

At first, though, Benito's mother worried because her child

remained silent at an age when most children were learning to talk. Fearing a handicap, she took him to a doctor. After an examination that revealed no physical problems, the doctor told Rosa, "Don't worry, he will speak. I have an idea he will speak too much."

And sure enough, at age three Benito began talking not just in one or two lisped words, but in complete sentences.

In 1885 another son, Arnaldo, had been born. A daughter, Edvige, was born three years later. In addition, Marianna, Rosa's mother, had joined the household. The Mussolinis had what their neighbors considered a large family. Perhaps too large. There were six of them, three adults and three children, crowded into a three-room apartment.

Benito and Arnaldo slept on a straw mat spread nightly on the floor of the small kitchen. The only heat came from a stove fueled with twigs that the boys gathered daily. Lunch was soup and hard bread. A salad of local greens was dinner. On Sundays the Mussolinis feasted on a pound of boiled mutton.

Encouraged by his father to fight, Benito grew into a violent boy, a bully.

Once, during harvesttime, an older boy stole Benito's toy cart. In tears, he ran to his father. "Men have to defend themselves, not ask for pity," Alessandro said sternly. "Don't come back to me again until you've licked him."

Still drying his tears, Benito found a piece of flint and sharpened it on a stone. Then, with the crude weapon clenched in his fist, he attacked his enemy with animal fury. He left the older boy bloody and submissive.

At the public school in the nearby town of Predappio, Benito fought almost daily. He made few friends.

He liked to spend his idle hours with "Old Joan," a fortuneteller who sold love potions and other quack remedies. She taught Benito some magic and made him respect his premonitions. Her influence lasted the rest of his life, leaving him superstitious and sensitive to omens.

Benito also spent hours reading. This, too, became a lifetime habit. He would often take a book or pamphlet from the storage chest in the room where he slept and wander off with it, reading all the time. He might disappear for hours, deep somewhere in a book. Sometimes he sprawled with a book on the back of an old plow horse. While the horse browsed across the fields, Benito read.

He would read the novels of Victor Hugo, his favorite author, aloud to anyone who would listen. Peasants who took advantage of this offer gathered in a barn to hear Benito's evening readings of Hugo's *Les Misérables*. Later, in the blacksmith shop, Benito read portions of Karl Marx's Socialist creed to his father's cronies.

Rosa wanted him to be a priest. She took him regularly to nearby San Cassiano, a church built in the ninth century. Benito pinched those passing in the aisle so savagely that he was soon banished from aisle seats. When Mass was over he often filled his pockets with acorns, got into a tree, and took potshots at any parishioners who stopped to chat with neighbors at the church door.

HE PLAYED MANY other pranks. Once, after filling his mouth with stolen cherries, he fell, twisting with apparent agony, in a crowded street. As the concerned people rushed to his aid, he let some of the cherry juice drip from his mouth like blood. Then, when the crowd was large enough to suit him, he jumped up, sprayed the bystanders with cherry juice, and ran away laughing.

Another time Benito organized a raid on a farmer's quince orchard. The venture almost ended tragically. The irate farmer fired a shotgun to scare the boys. In panic, one boy fell and broke his leg. While the others fled, Benito stood over his injured friend, scowling at the farmer. Then, as the man watched with gun cocked, Benito lifted his injured comrade onto his shoulders and carried him away.

Such deeds won Benito attention and even respect, two things he craved.

Although younger and gentler, Arnaldo was Benito's closest companion. The brothers went everywhere together. After school they roamed the countryside, stealing fruit and snaring small birds. But Benito's gentle moments were rare. He was known for his violence, his pranks, and his competitive spirit. When no one would race with him, he raced against himself, running around a village block while a man with a watch timed him. Young Benito never stopped trying to improve his speed.

Alessandro liked his son's spirit and thought he showed great promise, but Rosa had misgivings. Playing pranks, stealing fruit, snaring birds, and echoing the words of fortunetellers and revolutionaries were not, in her mind, promising traits. True, the boy was quick and clever, but he needed direction and discipline.

She decided to send him to private school. Alessandro objected strongly. Such schools were run by the Church. The boy would be indoctrinated with religion. Private education was not approved by Socialists, and besides, how could they pay for it?

Rosa overruled all Alessandro's objections, and at the age of nine, after yet another fight that had left the knuckles of his right hand scraped and bloody, Benito entered the Salesian school at Faenza, some twenty miles from home.

He hated it. He thought he was being punished. He saw the school as a prison and became an unruly inmate. Lessons bored him. He studied on his own and refused to do the assigned work. Punishment only made Benito more rebellious. Once, he was forced to kneel for four hours a day, twelve days in a row. After the tenth day his knees oozed blood from open sores. His teachers excused further punishment on the condition that Benito ask pardon for his sins. Benito refused to submit and finished the final two days of his ordeal.

On another occasion, he was forced to sleep outside in a courtyard where the school watchdogs prowled. One dog ripped the seat from his trousers and chased him over a gate, but Benito remained outside until dawn. During play periods, Benito had to stand alone, facing the wall, in a far corner of the school yard.

Whenever he joined the other boys, play turned to violence. The fighting was too much for the Salesian fathers. Near the end of his second year, after Benito stabbed an older boy in the buttocks with a pocketknife, the Mussolinis were asked to send their unruly child elsewhere.

The school records said Benito "is passionate and unruly; and he cannot adapt himself to the life of the school. . . . He places himself in opposition to every rule and discipline of the school. Nothing satisfies him; in the midst of so many people he feels more sad and more alone. . . . One personal motive guides him, and this is the principal streak in his character; he wishes to requite every injury inflicted by an older schoolmate. He cannot support an injury. He wants revenge. . . ."

Despite the school's opinion, Rosa continued to believe her oldest son deserved a private education. In October 1895 Benito entered the Royal Normal School at Forlimpopolo, just a few miles east of Varano di Costa. It was a happy choice.

Now twelve years old, he was perhaps a little wiser about dealing with other people. And the school was better, much better. It was run by Valfredo Carducci, a wise and gentle headmaster who won Benito's respect by encouraging the boy to continue studying independently as much as possible.

The school was full and at first Benito had to live with a family in town. This proved fortunate. Away from school, he could escape the hated routine and the temptation to fight with his schoolmates. His natural ambition to excel, encouraged by Carducci, soon turned Benito into a serious student. His best subjects were history, geography, and Italian literature, but he usually headed his class in all subjects.

In 1896 all Italy was shocked by the defeat of its army at

Adowa, a remote outpost in eastern Africa. A band of Abyssinian warriors left six thousand Italian dead and crushed Italy's colonial ambitions. Mussolini was only thirteen, but he felt the humiliation deeply. It made him more serious.

After three years at school, at the age of sixteen he was promoted to the senior class, given a small scholarship, and allowed to become a full-time boarder. He had by now achieved most of his growth. He was five feet six inches tall, with a thick, stocky body. His large, pale forehead was topped by thick, unruly hair. He had dark, penetrating eyes.

Although the black clothes he invariably wore had the green tarnish of age, he seemed proud of his outfit. He was particularly proud of the flowing black tie he wore as a symbol of his independent nature.

Benito sometimes took part in school games and discussions, but he seemed happiest when alone. Sometimes he retired to the tile rooftop of a nearby abandoned church in order to read undisturbed. Many times he forgot to come down for meals.

Though they respected him, most of his classmates avoided Benito. His stubborn pride, quick temper, and cutting wit made him a difficult companion. One classmate later described Benito Mussolini as "frankly disagreeable."

Benito's talents as an orator were obvious. On the playground, when he began voicing his views on politics or religion, he invariably drew a crowd. He also wrote occasional articles that were published by local political journals.

His teachers asked Mussolini to give the lead address at a public ceremony honoring Verdi, the great Italian composer. Benito used the occasion to blame current social conditions on the government.

Later, he upset school authorities by organizing a protest over the poor bread served the students. In another rebellion, he refused to do a history assignment because he needed all his time to study for an important geometry test. Carducci reluctantly suspended Benito for ten days.

Although he grew more and more impatient with school regulations and restrictions, Benito stayed until the end, receiving his diploma as a elementary school teacher in the summer of 1901. He was eighteen years old and ready to face the world. Or, at least, *he* thought he was ready.

2

Wandering

MUSSOLINI, who graduated on July 8, 1901, went home and applied for the job of town clerk in nearby Predappio. He was turned down.

Rosa, who had hoped the job might have given Benito respectability, or at least a new suit of clothes, was disappointed. Alessandro, convinced that his son would one day be famous, was furious. He appeared—a little drunk—before the Predappio town council.

"You'll be sorry you refused my son a job," he shouted, "but remember—even Crispi couldn't find a job in his own village."

The mayor and councilmen smiled at each other. The elder Mussolini was referring to Francesco Crispi, one of the most popular of Italy's founding fathers. The councilmen could see little resemblance between young Benito and their national hero.

The following day, Alessandro told Benito, "Your place is not here in this village, boy. Go out in the world. Take your place in the great fight."

Although he loved the village, Benito reluctantly agreed. Even Rosa, who was now in poor health and wanted her children near her, had to agree that there was little future for Benito in Varano di Costa—or any other small village.

At this time, Benito learned that Gualtieri, a town a hun-

12

dred miles to the northwest in Reggio Emilia Province, needed a teacher. He applied for the job and got it.

He arrived in Gualtieri wearing the same tarnished black suit he had worn in normal school, but the mayor and the headmaster welcomed the new teacher cordially. Soon parents of pupils began inviting him to their homes for dinner. Benito ignored the invitations, and the gossip started.

His revolutionary ideas soon became known, but they did not shock the town as much as his life-style. He spent his evenings drinking, dancing, playing cards, or arguing politics in noisy cafes. Sometimes, after too much wine, he would sleep with the town apprentices on the floor of a cobbler's shop.

When he did use his small room in Signora Panizzi's boarding house, he shocked the town by rising early, walking to the Po River, and bathing naked before the world. Wherever he walked, he carried his shoes peasant fashion, tied to a stick cocked over his shoulder. It saved shoe leather.

Despite his habits, Benito made friends among cafe companions and fellow teachers. In March of 1902 he was named to represent the school at a teachers' congress in Bologna. He had to borrow money to pay for the trip.

He was always broke. His job paid fifty-six lire a month, and forty of that went to Signora Panizzi for room and board. So Benito was not heartbroken when the town fathers decided not to renew his contract for another year. Gualtieri, it seemed, was not the arena for "the great fight."

Mussolini later denied that he left Italy to avoid military service, but the fact is that he left to seek his fortune in Switzerland just before he became eligible for the draft. Eventually, the Italian authorities added his name to the long list of deserters. Alessandro, an outspoken opponent of the compulsory draft, may have encouraged his son to emigrate. In any case, when Benito wrote home asking for the forty-five lire needed for a train ticket to Lausanne, Switzerland, his parents somehow found the money.

On July 9, 1902, Benito said farewell to Gualtieri. Cesare Gradella, a close friend, and Signora Panizzi's hunchbacked maid accompanied him to the station. The maid carried a bundle containing Benito's major purchase in Gualtieri—a new pair of shoes. After Benito boarded the train and found a window to wave farewell, the maid handed the shoes up to him. Benito took them with thanks, but when the train began to move, he tossed them back.

"Keep them as a souvenir," he called. "The luck of Mussolini won't hang on a pair of shoes."

He thought he would soon be earning ninety lire a month, enough to buy two pairs of shoes if he wished, but Switzerland was not the land of opportunity he had envisioned. After a thirty-six-hour train ride, he arrived in the town of Yverdon on the tenth of July. He had 2 lire and 10 centimes in his pocket. He described his experience in a letter to a friend.

"Feeling stupid and weary I made my way into a cheap-looking inn where I had occasion for the first time to speak French. I had something to eat. . . . On Saturday, together with an out-of-work painter, I went to Orbe, a neighboring town, to be taken on as a manual laborer. I found work and on Monday the fourteenth I began; eleven hours work in the day at 32 centesimi an hour. I made 121 journeys with a handbarrow full of stones up to the second floor of a building in process of construction. In the evening the muscles of my arms were swollen. I ate some potatoes roasted on cinders and threw myself in all my clothes onto my bed, a pile of straw. At five on Tuesday I woke and returned to work. I chafed with all the rage of the powerless. . . ."

Benito remained on the job until Saturday evening, when he asked for his pay—twenty lire and a few centimes.

Unfortunately, the work had worn his old shoes to tatters, and he was obliged to use most of his pay to buy a pair of sturdy boots. On Sunday, July 20, he took the train for Lausanne, arriving hungry and almost broke.

He searched for work, but no one would hire him. He slept in a packing case beneath a bridge and stole or begged for bread to stay alive. He was soon arrested as a vagrant. As his nineteenth birthday approached, he found himself in jail.

Meanwhile, his father had been arrested in Predappio, where frustrated Whites had smashed ballot boxes during an election that the Church-loving Blacks were sure to win. Benito heard of Alessandro's arrest but was unable to do anything about it.

There were six thousand Italians in Lausanne. Although many were laborers, many others were dodging Italian military service. It seemed that they all were poor, either unemployed or earning very low wages. Most Swiss despised the Italians and suspected them all of revolutionary ideas. And indeed, the suspicions were often true.

Socialism, by now an international movement, was popular among the Italian workers. Socialists embraced the ideas of Karl Marx, who urged redistribution of wealth to better the lot of the working class. They believed the time had come for redistribution, but disagreed on how it should be done. While some said the change could be brought about peacefully, many others, like Benito and his father, were convinced a revolution was necessary.

The Swiss police at first ignored Benito's politics and treated him lightly. He was released from jail after a short sentence and allowed to wander freely once more through the streets of Lausanne. In a cafe he met a friendly group of Italian Socialist bricklayers who treated him to a much-welcomed spaghetti dinner. Benito told them his background and described his revolutionary ideas.

His new friends soon found a job for him. Apparently it was not as demanding as the first one, and Benito was soon proudly signing his letters "Benito Mussolini, bricklayer."

Switzerland at this time was a haven for many political exiles from Russia. Mussolini met and accepted the hospitality of many Russians. He found most of them intelligent and stimulating. He thought the Russian girls were very attractive and tried to seduce them at every opportunity.

Most of his time and energy, however, were spent organizing Socialists. He was soon elected secretary of the Italian Trade Union of Bricklayers and Bricklayers' Assistants, and he was invariably chosen to speak to striking and demonstrating workers. This gave Mussolini's natural talents as an orator a chance to mature. He could capture the emotion of a crowd, build it, and play with it like a conductor with a symphony orchestra. He learned the importance of pace and volume; he practiced gestures. He loved the cheers and the attentive faces of his listeners.

But he was not always on the podium. While in the crowd of listeners at a Socialist meeting, he came to the attention of Angelica Balabanoff. A member of a wealthy Russian family, she had gone to Italy to study, but soon moved to Switzerland to help Italian workers. During one of her many speeches she noticed Mussolini in the audience.

> "He was a young man I had never seen before," she recalled, "and his agitated manner and unkempt clothes set him apart from the other workers in the hall. The emigré audiences were always poorly dressed, but this man was also extremely dirty. I had never seen a more wretched human being. In spite of his large jaw, and the bitterness and restlessness in the black eyes, he gave the impression of extreme timidity. Even as he listened, his nervous hands clutching at his big black hat, he seemed more concerned with his inner turmoil than with what I was saying."

After the meeting, Angelica talked to Benito and asked him to help her translate a German political pamphlet into Italian. She could pay him a few lire for the work. Benito accepted. It was the start of a friendship that would last several years.

Angelica had no illusions about Benito's character. She later wrote:

> "I soon saw that he knew little of history, of economics, or of Socialist theory and that his mind was completely undisciplined. . . . Mussolini's radicalism and anticlericalism were more the reflection of his early environment and his own rebellious egotism than the product of understanding and conviction. His hatred of oppression was not that impersonal hatred of a system shared by all revolutionaries. It sprang from his own sense of indignity and frustration, his passion to assert his own ego, and from a determination for personal revenge."

Under Angelica's guidance, Benito did try to learn more about the history and theory of socialism. He attended lectures and read philosophy. At one lecture, however, he rose to take issue with the speaker, who claimed that Jesus Christ was history's first Socialist. Encouraged by his friends, Benito challenged Christianity and praised Buddhism, which he knew nothing about. The speaker, adept at handling hecklers, soon had the crowd roaring with laughter at Benito's ignorance.

The experience taught Benito a lesson. Later, when he rose to debate the reality of God with a Lausanne preacher, Benito borrowed a cheap pocket watch from a friend and held it up dramatically before the crowd.

"It is now 3:30 P.M.," he said. "If God exists, I give him five minutes to strike me dead."

When nothing happened to the defiant young man, the crowd roared its approval. The preacher had no rebuttal for such theatrics. Swiss authorities, however, heard about the incident and decided Benito Mussolini was an unwelcome atheist. The police ordered him to leave the country.

Benito crossed the border into France, where he worked as a laborer and part-time teacher in a private school. The wife of the assistant headmaster, finding that Benito could tell her fortune, became his lover. She encouraged him to stay in France, but Benito had the urge to wander.

He went to Zurich, where the Swiss authorities did not yet know him. But he was soon frequenting Socialist meetings and once again inviting attention. A political brawl in a restaurant brought a request from police for Mussolini to leave the country.

He went to Germany, where he worked briefly as a mason. Then, early in 1903, he managed to enter Switzerland again. He settled in Berne, where he soon persuaded the masons to strike. Cautious members of the union tried to restrict Mussolini's activities. He called them cowards. One mason resented the insult so much that he challenged Mussolini to a duel. It was fought with pistols. Neither man was hit, but the incident drew attention from Berne police.

In October of that year, once again on police orders, Mussolini left Switzerland. This time he went home to visit Rosa, who was now gravely ill. Although he was devoted to his mother, Benito did not have the patience to sit for long at anyone's bedside. He wanted to travel again, and the moment Rosa showed slightly improved health, Benito headed for the station.

He took the train to Annemasse to visit his French mistress. While there he prepared a false passport for Switzerland, but it did not fool the border police. He was imprisoned and then deported.

Listed by now as a deserter from Italian military service, Benito could not go home without being arrested. So he returned to Annemasse where he plotted once again to enter Switzerland. Near the end of 1904 he managed to get into Lausanne, but his stay was cut short by interesting news from Italy. King Victor

Emmanuel III signed a royal degree granting amnesty to all deserters who presented themselves for military duty.

For Benito Mussolini, the timing was perfect. Tired of wandering, he could now return to his homeland without being imprisoned. And he could replace his shabby black suit with the uniform of an Italian soldier.

3

The Journalist

MILITARY LIFE agreed with Mussolini. It was remarkable that the rebel, in conflict with authority for most of his twenty-one years, adjusted to the army with so little complaint.

He was assigned to the 10th Bersaglieri Rifle Regiment stationed at Verona, 130 miles north of home. The regiment was famous for its quick-jog marching pace and its round hats decorated with long green feathers. Benito was proud of the regiment. And to his surprise, he was proud of his country.

Two unhappy years of wandering had planted the seeds of patriotism. It was a case of absence making his heart grow fonder of both country and friends.

Of course, among his Socialists friends, he could not dwell on patriotism. Socialism, a worldwide movement, recognized no national boundaries. To be a Socialist one must forget one's country and give allegiance to the movement.

The army, however, gave Mussolini a holiday from political dogma. His duties as a private were easy, and home leave was granted regularly. When home he spent happy days helping in his father's shop. In the evenings, father and son sat before the kitchen fire and read to each other.

Their favorite book was *The Prince*, by Niccolo Machiavelli, the sixteenth-century Italian statesman and cynical philosopher who placed political expediency above morality.

"This may be said generally of men," Machiavelli wrote in a typical passage, "that they are ungrateful, voluble, deceitful, shirkers of dangers, greedy of gain."

Machiavelli advised those who would rule that it was better to be feared than loved.

Twenty years later, in recalling these reading sessions, Mussolini said Machiavelli's views impressed him because they paralleled his own so closely.

In February 1905, Private Mussolini received word that his mother was dying of meningitis. He rushed home, arriving just before Rosa breathed her last. Later Mussolini wrote, "From me had been taken the one dear and truly near living being."

He returned sadly to Verona, completed the remaining nineteen months of his military service without incident, and returned to civilian life. In September 1906 he was home again, twenty-three years old, restless, and unemployed.

After a brief love affair with the school teacher who had replaced his mother, he took a teaching job at Caneva, a small town in northeastern Italy. He was bored, lonely, and homesick. The northern winter was long and cold. He yearned for some other profession, anything but teaching.

His radical politics provided some excitement. After Benito attacked the government in a speech, Caneva police threatened to arrest him. Later, he was accused of using blasphemy in the classroom. To no one's surprise and to his delight, his contract was not renewed at the end of the school year.

Meanwhile, from Oneglia on the Italian Riviera, a friend wrote with a fascinating plan. The friend needed an editor to help start a Socialist paper. There was little pay, but a private school nearby needed a French teacher.

It took Mussolini little more than six months of hard study to know French well enough to pass an examination that qualified him to teach the language. He then applied for the job in Oneglia and was accepted.

He arrived in time to bring out the first issue of *La Lima*, his friend's weekly paper. Then he settled into a routine of teaching French by day and working on the paper at night. The police of Oneglia, who knew of Mussolini's radical politics, objected, and the police chief asked the headmaster to dismiss the new French teacher. The headmaster refused and told Mussolini about the incident.

He was delighted and used the pages of *La Lima* to attack the police. He also lashed out at the Church and the government. Priests and town leaders were outraged, but the louder they complained, the bolder Mussolini's attacks. He loved it. He had found himself at last. He was not meant to be a teacher; he was meant to be a radical journalist.

By June of 1908, however, the police had had enough. They ordered Mussolini to leave Oneglia as soon as possible. He wrote a defiant farewell in his last edition of the paper:

"In a few days I shall go and in order that you may be able to report me, I now inform you of my exact address: the house close to the fifteen-kilometer stone on the provincial road on the river Rabbi, hamlet of Dovia, commune Predappio, province of Forli. Make note of it and try to see whether it is possible also to drive me out of my father's house."

Home had changed in his absence. His father had sold the blacksmith shop and remarried. He and his new wife, Anna Guidi, had moved to nearby Forli to manage a combination inn and wine parlor. Rachele, Anna's sixteen-year-old daughter from an earlier marriage, was helping behind the bar.

She was a shy country girl, pretty but also hardy. She had worked as a goatherd and farmhand, and she had known Benito Mussolini since she was seven years old. She had always admired him. Now he flirted with her and she encouraged him.

Anna and his father were disgusted. Mussolini had a bad reputation with women. He had seduced at least eight girls in the district. Anna and Alessandro both warned Rachele, but it was too late. She was in love.

Mussolini did not let the affair interfere with politics. Before he had been home a month, he was sentenced to a short jail term for disturbing the peace. Later, he was fined one hundred lire for urging rebellion in a public speech. And before 1908 came to a close, he wrote a newspaper article attacking the conservative faction of the Socialist party. The article caused a great stir and threatened to split the party. Just the same, soon after the new year, he was offered another job on a Socialist newspaper.

The offer came from Trent, then part of Austria. He did not want to leave Italy, but he could not miss an opportunity to further his career in journalism. Actually, his title would be secretary of Trent's Chamber of Labor, but his major duty would be editing *L'Avvenire del Lavoratore,* a Socialist newspaper published weekly by the Chamber.

Before boarding the train for the 150-mile journey to Trent, he promised Rachele that they would be married the day he returned. Rachele laughed. She knew that Socialists were opposed to religion of any kind and that any Socialist who went to church and knelt before a priest even to be married risked expulsion from the party.

Trent was a disappointment. It was not an industrial city, and the large working class Mussolini had counted on for an audience did not exist. Most of Trent's Socialists endorsed the moderate policies that Mussolini opposed.

His enthusiasm, however, overcame the disappointment. The pages of *L'Avvenire* were soon crackling with revolutionary declarations and attacks on the authorities. The Church and the local Catholic newspaper became his major targets. He also contributed articles to *Popolo,* a daily newspaper published in

Vienna by Cesare Battista, one of Austria's leading Socialists. Battista's friendship and moderate nature had a beneficial influence on Mussolini.

But in the beginning, the new editor of *L'Avvenire* was anything but moderate. He called priests in the Vatican "a gang of robbers" and a popular local priest a mad dog. The editor of the local Catholic paper, Mussolini said, could not be described in a family newspaper. An Austrian court fined him for these outrages and later locked him in jail for eight days after he wrote an article urging all Italians living in Austria to rebel. Five other jail sentences followed.

In August 1909, soon after his release from one of these sentences, Battista asked him to edit *Popolo*. He expected Mussolini to retain the paper's moderate character. Battista was an Italian patriot, not at all committed to the international flavor of socialism. Also, he opposed revolution.

Mussolini took the new job. He had no qualms about editing both papers simultaneously. In *L'Avvenire*, he continued to urge international revolt. In *Popolo*, he followed Battista's moderate tone. Soon, as if the two editorial jobs were not enough, Mussolini began contributing pieces of fiction to *La Vita Trentina*, a weekly supplement of *Popolo*. One of these serial stories, "Claudia Particella or the Cardinal's Love," was later published as a novel called *The Cardinal's Mistress*. It was not a best-seller, but it allowed Mussolini to vent some of his religious hatred.

The Austrian police harassed him constantly. They banned eleven different issues of *L'Avvenire*, but they could not silence the revolutionary editor.

Finally, in September of 1909, after a bank robbery in Trent, the Austrian police took decisive action and arrested Mussolini. There was no proof linking him to the robbery, but the police deported him on the ground that his paper may have encouraged the crime.

The deportation added to Mussolini's reputation as a fearless revolutionary. He had barely returned to home soil when he was offered a job as chapter secretary for the Socialist party in nearby Forli. The job paid 120 lire a month, more than Mussolini had ever earned before. He could pay the rent on an apartment and have enough left over to start his own newspaper. He accepted the job at once, and within a few days the first issue of *La Lotta di Classe* (The Class Struggle) appeared in Forli. Thus, he started the year 1910 as an independent publisher.

The radical nature of the paper attracted immediate attention from the authorities. The police regarded the young editor as a threat to the political stability of the entire district.

Meanwhile, Mussolini and Rachele moved into a two-room apartment in Forli and began living together as man and wife. As Rachele suspected, there was no wedding ceremony.

Alessandro warned that Benito's politics would bring the couple nothing but grief. Benito's answer was typical. He produced a revolver and glared at his father, saying, "Here are six bullets—one for Rachele and five for me."

Alessandro shrugged. Further protest was useless.

Although Mussolini roused the ire of Church and government leaders, Forli was not a hotbed of revolution. Most people were Republicans opposed to the monarchy but in favor of the existing Senate and Chamber of Deputies of Italy's parliamentary system. The few Socialists in and around Forli were political outcasts.

Circulation of *La Lotta di Classe* never exceeded 350 copies a week, but it managed to rouse the hostile attention of nearly everyone in the district, including the moderate Socialists who opposed violence and revolution. Mussolini called them cowards.

In some cases the moderates feared and hated Mussolini more than Forli's Republicans. Mussolini was delighted. Like Machiavelli, he believed more could be achieved out of fear than out of love, and his attacks brought him attention. That was what he most wanted.

On September 1, 1910, the eighteen-year-old Rachele gave birth to their first child, a daughter, Edda. The fifteen lire in the family cashbox was barely enough to pay for a cradle.

Two months later, Alessandro died at the age of fifty-seven. All of the three thousand Socialists attending the burial agreed that the party had suffered a great loss.

His father's death pained him deeply, but Mussolini had little time to mourn. In addition to his newspaper duties, he spent hours trying to reorganize and revitalize the party. When he was not giving speeches or urging factory workers to unite, he was tramping about the country, visiting tenant farmers and laborers.

Mussolini was always broke. He owned just one pair of trousers. When they were being washed, he was forced to stay home. For his lunches, he earned a ham sandwich by sitting behind a newsstand counter while the proprietor went home for lunch.

He watched food prices daily, and when the town council approved a slight increase in the cost of milk, he immediately organized a gang of workers and led them, shouting angrily, to the city hall. Mussolini soon stood before the mayor of Forli.

"Either the price of milk is revised," he told His Honor, "or I'll advise these people to pitch you and all your bigwigs over the balcony."

The milk went back to its previous price.

Although he rarely drank hard liquor, when he did Mussolini invariably got roaring drunk. Soon after Edda was born, he came staggering home at 5 A.M. one day and began smashing every piece of pottery in the apartment. When he awoke nine hours later, Rachele told him, "If you ever come home again like that, I'll kill you!"

Mussolini swore off hard liquor for the rest of his life.

In September 1911, after the Italian army invaded Libya on the North African coast, Mussolini followed the Socialist party line and opposed the government's war policies.

Actually, Italy risked little in the venture. Turkey, which had controlled Libya, had lost its power throughout the Mediterranean. Italy was simply taking over a colony that the Turks were ready to abandon.

The Libyan venture appealed to Mussolini's patriotism, but he could not admit it. He urged active opposition to the war, culminating his campaign with an eloquent speech that sparked a riot in Forli. Railway tracks were torn up, buses overturned, and streets barricaded. Government troops were called in to restore order. When the dust cleared, Mussolini stood behind bars, convicted on eight charges of inciting a riot. He was sentenced to a year in jail, but he appealed and used the new trial as a political platform. In his defense, he struck a moderate tone that won national attention.

At one point he declared, "I have written and said what I have written and said, because I want and love an Italy that is conscious of her duty, and struggles to redeem her people from economic and spiritual misery rather than violate the homeland of others in order to extend to it her own pauperism."

Mussolini's appeal drew applause both in court and out. In the end, despite the prosecutor's warning that such a clever speaker was dangerous, the court reduced the sentence from a year to five months.

When Mussolini emerged from jail, Socialists everywhere hailed him as a hero. At a banquet in his honor, Olindo Vernocchi, a party veteran, declared, "From today you, Benito, are not only the representative of the Romagna Socialists but the Duke (*Il Duce*, in Italian) of all revolutionary Socialists in Italy."

It was the first time he was called *Il Duce*, but the title stuck the rest of his life. Pronounced "Dew-chay," the word would one day become a national chant.

4

The Politician

AT AGE TWENTY-NINE, still pale from prison, Mussolini was asked to speak before a national congress of Socialists. His appearance alone made a memorable impression.

"I found myself," Socialist Cesare Rossi recalled, "in the presence of a man with a thin, emaciated, bony face and a thick beard of several days' growth. He wore a gray, wide-brimmed hat of Romagnole design, which was threadbare and greasy. His jacket, which had originally been black, had become green with use. His pockets were full of newspapers. He wore an incredibly worn-out flowing tie, a shirt and collar that should have been white but had not been so for a long time, a pair of old fustian trousers with crumpled knees showing long service and disdain for the ironing board, and a pair of shoes that had not known polish for months."

The moment he stepped to the podium the delegates rose to their feet, cheering. Without question, he was the hero of the party.

Mussolini used his newfound stature to widen the split between the moderate and the revolutionary factions of the party. With his dramatic speaking style, he was able to turn a small incident into a national issue.

It happened that a would-be assassin had shot at but missed King Victor Emmanuel III. The moderate leaders of the

Socialist party had sent the king a message, congratulating him on his survival. Mussolini, his words snapping in rapid bursts, angrily condemned the message and the men who had sent it. He said all Socialists must work to eliminate, not encourage, monarchs.

"What is a king, anyway, except by definition a useless citizen? There are people who have sent their king packing; others even have preferred to take the precaution of sending him to the guillotine, and those peoples are in the vanguard of progress."

The delegates were so roused by Mussolini's speech that they voted four moderate leaders out of the party. The editor of *Avanti* (Forward), the Socialists' national daily, published in Milan, was one of those dismissed. Although control of the paper went to someone else, Mussolini made it known that he would one day like to have the job.

The day was not long in coming. A few months after the close of the national congress, he received news that the job was open again. Would he take it?

He accepted at once, and one of his first steps as editor of a national paper was to appoint Angelica Balabanoff, his Russian friend from the vagabond days, as his assistant. Then he and his family moved to Milan.

The city, already Italy's major industrial center, was ripe for Mussolini's brand of revolutionary socialism. Hunger, poverty, housing shortages, labor unrest, and all the other social problems caused by Italy's slow but steady advance into the twentieth century were focused in Milan.

After settling Rachele and Edda in a downtown apartment, Mussolini gave all his energy to the paper. He sensed what people wanted to read. He made the paper lively and interesting. Although his editorials and articles were often full of errors and contradictions, his forceful style compelled readership.

Almost overnight, the circulation of *Avanti* jumped from 20,000 to 100,000.

Many disagreed with Mussolini, but everyone seemed to read his paper. Often it was hard to say what he believed. His editorials and speeches were tuned to the public attitudes of the moment. It was not what he said but how he said it that made Mussolini interesting.

Mussolini was consistent in urging revolution, and the possibility of revolt grew daily. In 1913 new riots in southern Italy were suppressed only after troops opened fire on the crowds, killing and wounding hundreds of citizens. The unrest spread and soon talk of mass protests was heard everywhere.

Late in the year Mussolini ran for Parliament on the Socialist party ticket to represent Forli. Although the dominant Republican registration in his home district promised defeat, Mussolini campaigned so vigorously for other Socialist candidates that the party won fifty-three seats in the Chamber of Deputies, far more than expected.

In March 1914, after riots broke out in northern Italy, police arrested Mussolini on charges of encouraging unrest. At his trial, he again used the courtroom as a platform to voice his revolutionary ideas. After hearing two weeks of his oratory, the jury voted for acquittal.

Now the most famous Socialist in Italy, Mussolini decided to test the party's strength. He organized a national day of protest over the treatment of jailed Socialists and other political prisoners. Mussolini said that any attempt to suppress the protest must be answered with a general strike.

The protest, held on June 7, passed peacefully everywhere except in Ancona, a port city on the Adriatic Sea. Police fired into a crowd, killing three and wounding ten citizens. Immediately, the Socialist party ordered the general strike. The strike fizzled. Although workers stayed home for a few days, they were not prepared to survive long without pay. Meanwhile, the government threatened to use the army to restore public services. Union leaders had no choice but to order everyone back to their jobs.

Although Mussolini tried to blame moderate Socialists for the strike's collapse, he knew that he had seriously over-estimated his party's strength. Unarmed men could not be asked to confront government troops. In the future Mussolini would be far more cautious.

In June 1914 he ran for Parliament again, this time to represent Milan. He won easily and took his seat in the Chamber of Deputies in time to debate the question that would divide Italy: War or peace?

THE WAR BEGAN in August 1914, after Archduke Ferdinand of Austria-Hungary was assassinated at Sarajevo in what is now Yugoslavia. The war grew into a huge struggle among nations over the control of Europe. Basically, it pitted Germany and Austria-Hungary, the "Central Powers," against England and France, the "Western Allies."

Italy, with no weight in the balance of power, tried to be neutral. For once, the country's policy paralleled Socialist policy. As a leading Socialist, Mussolini found himself in the uncomfortable position of agreeing with the government.

There were two practical reasons for staying out of the war. Italy was not prepared to fight, and even if she were, she could not decide which side to join.

In the last century Austria-Hungary had defeated Italy and taken border cities such as Trent, which had large populations of Italian-speaking people. Now, if Italy joined the Allies and they won, she might win back cities and territories as spoils of victory. On the other hand, Italy also had claims on French border cities. If Italy joined the Central Powers and they won, she might gain cities and territories from France.

The debate seemed endless. Mussolini at first argued stoutly for neutrality, but as the weeks passed and the intensity of the war grew, he began to have doubts.

Austria-Hungary, with its monarchy and old-fashioned aristocratic capitalism, represented all the things Mussolini opposed. Certainly it would be better to side with France, a progressive republic, than it would be to side with the tired, old empire. The war also revived the spirit of patriotism that had surprised Mussolini while serving in the army. To the patriotic spirit he added national ambition. If Italy were to take its rightful place in the European community, it would have to choose sides. But which side would win?

At first, Germany's well-trained army seemed unbeatable, but then came the Battle of the Marne, just outside Paris. In four bloody September days, the French stopped the German advance. The battle upset the Central Powers' timetable of conquest and brought the deadly stalemate of trench warfare to the western front.

Mussolini, now believing the Central Powers would eventually lose, began to dream of a larger Italy that embraced all disputed Austrian territory. He continued publicly to favor neutrality, but privately spoke to friends of the advantages of joining the Allies.

On October 10, 1914, however, he wrote an editorial in *Avanti* suggesting that Italy adopt a policy of "armed neutrality." Socialists howled in protest, but Mussolini sensed that the majority of public opinion favored his stand. Indeed, socialism was losing its popularity largely because of its neutrality. Soon the pages of *Avanti* were urging armed intervention in every issue.

His enemies accused Mussolini of changing his position in exchange for French bribes. At first he denied taking any money from the French, but he later admitted accepting "loans." He was never able to prove, however, that the money was repaid.

Meanwhile, in an emergency meeting of the Socialist Central Committee, he was dismissed from *Avanti*. He said nothing in his defense and refused an offer of salary extension until he found another job.

Mussolini already knew what his next job would be. He would start his own paper. He had dreamed of it for a long time. It would free him from the restrictive party line. Although most of his financial backing undoubtedly came from France, he did not think he was selling himself. After all, he had already decided Italy should join the Allies.

Judging from the office of his new paper, France was not making him rich. He rented the attic of an old building in Milan's red-light district and furnished it with one chair, one desk, and some wooden crates to seat visitors. At the moment he wanted no company. He put a sign over the attic door: IF YOU ENTER, YOU'LL DO ME AN HONOR; IF YOU STAY OUT, YOU'LL DO ME A FAVOR.

The first issue of *Il Popolo d'Italia* (The People of Italy) appeared on November 15, 1914. It was subtitled "A Socialist Daily," but the masthead carried such non-Socialist slogans as "He who has steel has bread" and "A revolution is an idea that has found bayonets." Furthermore, the lead article of the first issued appealed to the young men of Italy to go to war.

Socialists were stunned.

Despite all his planning, Mussolini had not anticipated the violence of the reaction. He expected that his popularity and his persuasive talents as a journalist and orator would eventually bring party policy in line with his own views. He did not want to break from the party. The Socialists, however, were too angry to listen to persuasion.

They called a hasty meeting in an old Milan theater and demanded that Mussolini appear and explain himself. It was an angry crowd. The moment he stepped on the stage he was greeted with catcalls, boos, and cries of "Traitor! Judas! Assassin!" Then the chanting began. "Who's paying? Who's paying?"

His appeal for silence went unheard. Small coins rained down on the stage. He had to jump to avoid a flying chair.

Suddenly, in a fit of rage, he snatched up a drinking glass, held it aloft, and crushed it in his fist. The dramatic gesture did little to silence the crowd. The din continued as water and blood ran down Mussolini's wrist.

"You hate me because you still love me," he shouted, but only those nearby heard him. Then, white with anger, he left the stage and strode up an aisle and out of the theater.

He rushed to his attic office and began writing with the energy of hate. His paper attacked all who opposed Italy's intervention in the war, especially Socialists. Circulation rose at once.

Mussolini's timing had been faultless. Public opinion as well as government policy were shifting toward intervention on the side of the Allies. By March 1915, less than four months after it first appeared, *Il Popolo d'Italia* could boast a circulation of one hundred thousand.

Mussolini, however, had made some lasting enemies. More than one evening on his way home from work, he had to dodge rocks and bottles thrown from windows and dark alleys. Although he showed little regard for personal safety, his response to the attacks harkened back to his childhood. It was necessary to get even. He urged the formation of gangs to demonstrate against neutrality. He called these gangs *fascio,* a word used to describe any group of political activists. It was to gain new meaning, however, as Mussolini's power grew. From it rose the word *fascism* to describe Mussolini's brand of politics through violence. The name also led to the choice of a symbol, the *fasces,* or bundle of rods surrounding an ax, which was once used by Roman emperors as the symbol of office.

In Rome he joined one of his newly organized *fascio* in a pro-war demonstration. He and several others were arrested, but after eight hours, they were released without charge.

Meanwhile, the Italian government was secretly negotiating with both sides in the war. To Austria, Italy offered to remain neutral in exchange for at least some of the disputed border territory. Austria managed to keep Italy out of the war for many months by prolonging the negotiations.

Negotiations with the English were more promising. At meetings in London, Italian ambassadors said their country would join the Allies if it could be assured the disputed Austrian territories as a condition of victory.

The English not only agreed to give Italy South Tyrol, Gorizia, Gradisca, Istria, and Trieste, but also promised the Adriatic islands of Cherso and Lussino, a big chunk of the Dalmation coast that is now part of Yugoslavia, and fifty million English pounds. Italy was further assured participation in the division of Asia Minor after the war.

Italy declared war on the Central Powers on May 24, 1915.

Il Popolo d'Italia hailed the news as a personal triumph for Il Duce. And because the promises made in London remained secret until after the war, Mussolini's role in bringing his country into the war did indeed seem larger than it really was.

5

Birth of Fascism

CALLED TO ACTIVE DUTY at the end of August 1915, Mussolini hurried to join the 11th Bersaglieri Regiment, which was then in the trenches of the Austrian frontier high in the Italian Alps.

The three months that had passed since Italy's entry into the war had given Mussolini ample time to prepare the staff of *Il Popolo d'Italia* for his absence. He had put Guiseppe de Falco, a veteran newsman, in charge. The new editor's breezy and entertaining style gave a flair to the paper that it had earlier lacked. Eventually, seeing de Falco as a threat to his own popularity, Mussolini was to fire him without warning. But this came later.

When Private Mussolini joined his regiment, the fighting against Austria had already stalled in Alpine trenches. Daily rifle fire and canon barrages had created a deadly stalemate. The main enemies for the soldiers, however, were freezing cold, mud, hunger, thirst, and boredom.

Occasionally, officers came by and asked to be introduced to the famous editor from Milan. Mussolini could have asked for easier service, but he stayed in the trenches. All he wanted was help in getting his weekly reports to his paper, and this was readily provided. Readers of *Il Popolo d'Italia* thus learned the realities of trench warfare.

Hunched in a bunker, writing by the light of a sardine oil lamp, he described the alpine winds that froze the ground almost every night. If a man did not keep moving he risked having his boots locked in the grip of frozen mud. Water was so scarce and washing so difficult that the men became infested with lice. On warm days the air turned sickly sweet with the smell of bodies rotting in the no-man's land between the trenches.

When the Austrian shells sometimes pinned them down, making it impossible to reach field kitchens, the men went hungry. In one long barrage Mussolini and his comrades cooked and ate straw. He described all this and more in his reports. He also wrote anonymous articles encouraging greater war effort.

Near the end of 1915 Mussolini had a mild case of typhoid fever and was sent home to recuperate. Unable to adjust to the soft bed in his apartment, he slept on the floor. Actually, he spent little time trying to sleep. Domestic problems kept him very busy.

In September, Rachele had given birth to their second child, a boy called Vittorio Alessandro. A few weeks later, Ida Dalser, a Milan beauty parlor operator, also gave birth to a boy. She called him Benito, claimed Mussolini was the father, and demanded that he marry her. Mussolini admitted the child was his but refused to marry the woman.

Instead, in a civil ceremony held on December 16, 1915, he married Rachele. Meanwhile, to further complicate his life, he began a long-lasting affair with Margherita Sarfatti, the art critic on his newspaper.

Back at the front in February 1916, he told a friend that he was so sick of women that it would be a relief to face the Austrians again.

He resumed a life on the front of bare survival and eventually won promotion to lance sergeant, but by then his military career was almost over.

On February 22, 1917, three weeks after his promotion, Mussolini and nineteen others were blown out of their gunpit when an overheated howitzer exploded. Four men were killed instantly. Others lay stunned and bleeding. Mussolini, found fifteen feet from the blast, was so riddled with gun splinters that he was almost given up for dead.

Doctors in a field hospital removed forty-four pieces of steel, but there were other pieces they could not reach. Infection was unavoidable. Mussolini's temperature rose to 103 degrees and hung there for hours. It seemed hopeless. Festering wounds, some as large as a man's fist, marked splinters that still had to be removed. During the next month, doctors operated twenty-six more times. Six months passed before he was strong enough to get out of bed and walk a few steps.

While in the hospital, he was visited by King Victor Emmanuel III, once the frequent target of Il Duce's editorial attacks. Mussolini was now grateful for the royal attention.

He returned to Milan in August of 1917. Still on crutches, his appearance shocked everyone.

"He was so exhausted," Margherita Sarfatti recalled, "that he could scarcely speak. He smiled out at us from his pale face, his eyes sunken in great hollows. His lips scarcely moved; one could see how horribly he had suffered. Someone asked him if he would like a book to read. He refused. . . ."

His large dark eyes were now the most dominant features in his pale, thin face.

His character had also changed. He was more mature and more confident. He no longer needed his ragged suit and floppy hat to get attention. He now wore a trim dark suit and a white shirt with a stiff collar. He shaved daily.

His talents as a journalist and an orator were more polished. As soon as he began to recover his health, he drew heavily on these talents, mainly to defend himself.

The war was proving longer and more costly than anyone had expected, and Italian pacifists blamed Mussolini for all the bloodshed. The pacifist cause received a tremendous lift when

Pope Benedict XV appealed for a separate treaty with the Central Powers.

Mussolini attacked all pacifists, including the pope. In editorials and speeches Mussolini appealed to patriotism and fanned new flames of hatred for the enemy. He thrived on this activity. The pacifists were losing ground in the war of words until October 1917, when shocking news came the front. Austria had crushed an Italian army at Caporetto (Kobarid), in what is now Yugoslavia.

The disaster demoralized the nation, and it did not help when the Italian general in charge blamed his troops for the defeat. In time, however, the country gradually rallied, and Mussolini, sensing the revival, launched a timely campaign supporting the government and calling for discipline and renewed effort.

What happened to his antigovernment role? "Political liberty is for a time of peace," he explained. "In time of war it is treason."

He accused Socialists of treason and urged that Socialist newspapers be suppressed. Hope of reconciliation with his old party dimmed. At the moment, he did not want it. As a lone wolf, with no party line to follow, he was free to adjust his views to fit the popular mood of the moment.

Meanwhile, the Italian army, with support from France and England, gained enough strength to win a decisive victory in the alpine foothills. It was Italy's last battle of the war. In November 1918 the Austro-Hungarian forces surrendered. A few days later Germany asked for peace.

For Italy there was little to celebrate. The war had left the country in serious trouble. Raw materials were depleted. The merchant fleet was in shambles. Soldiers returning from the front expecting a better life could not find jobs. Thousands were out of work. The government was bankrupt.

Meanwhile, the Allies all but ignored the promises made

to Italy in London. Only a few acres were actually granted Italy in postwar treaties. Italians, their pride crushed, felt they had been betrayed. Had their 652,000 war dead made a vain sacrifice?

In desperation many people turned to communism, a revolutionary brand of socialism that had guided the bloody overthrow of Russia's tsarist government in 1917. Generally, communism was more of a fear than a threat; socialism, however, gained followers by the thousands.

Postwar Italy was soon divided between those on the Left who advocated socialism, communism, or some other drastic change, and those on the Right who wanted to retain the traditional forms of government and society. The Left included the pacifists who now charged that Mussolini and other advocates of war were responsible for most of the country's problems. The Right included the patriotic nationalists who defended the war. Almost all returning veterans were nationalists.

As a wounded veteran and advocate of the war, Mussolini found himself often on the Right, but he still attacked the government. Italy, he said, should ignore the treaties and simply annex the territories that had been promised. In the January 1, 1919, edition of *Il Popolo d'Italia* he outlined a plan for the occupation of Fiume (now Rijeka) as the first step in taking possession of the Dalmatian coast.

Meanwhile, after the Communists staged a noisy demonstration in Milan, Mussolini decided to reactivate the *fascio,* the militialike squads that had been so effective earlier in silencing war opponents. In his paper he urged all interested in joining to attend a meeting on March 23, 1919, in a public auditorium on Milan's Piazza San Sepolcro.

Although no more than 150 men attended, the event was later hailed as the beginning of the Fascist party.

Mussolini did the talking. He spoke for women's voting rights, benefits for veterans, an eight-hour maximum workday, and all-out war against Communists and Socialists. Those attending voted to demand the annexation of Dalmatia, and they decided to call themselves *Fasci di Combattimento,* or "squads of combat."

Wanting the liberty to change his views, Mussolini avoided a detailed party line for the *fascio.* He had to test public opinion and adjust to it. Sometimes he liked to write or say something outrageous simply to get attention. It was a shifting game. When he attacked the government, he stood on the Left. When he attacked socialism, he stood on the Right.

The June 6, 1919, issue of *Il Popolo d'Italia* finally listed the goals of fascism. They included

- the revision of the election laws so that all those eighteen and older could vote;
- the establishment of minimum wages and an eight-hour day;
- the formation of government councils to administer health, welfare, education, and other social benefits;
- the confiscation of all Church property;
- the reorganization of rail and other transport to improve service;
- the creation of a national militia that would reduce the cost of a standing army;
- the government takeover of munitions factories; and
- the pursuit of a foreign policy that would enable Italy to take her proper place in the peaceful competition between civilized nations.

Coming from Mussolini, the list seemed mild. It attracted little attention or excitement.

What did stimulate his followers was the hate campaign he unleashed at this time against the "rich nations," particularly France and England. He blamed both countries for Italy's postwar poverty. His attack boosted his popularity, particularly among his fellow veterans.

He went to Fiume and spoke to a crowd of veterans in the old Verdi theater. When he attacked England and France, the cheering almost brought down the rafters. Mussolini loved the sound. He then said that Tunisia in North Africa should be liberated from France. The crowd roared approval. He said the Island of Malta should be liberated from England. The crowd exploded. He said Egypt should be helped to expel all foreigners. The theater rocked with noise. He said the Mediterranean should be turned into an Italian Sea. Thunder!

The same speech, or one very much like it, was repeated in other theaters in other cities. It roused the same cheering. And so Mussolini's pattern was set. He attacked the foreign capitalism of England and France. He played on the fear of communism and used the *fascio* to threaten his foes with violence. Fascism thus grew into a political force that had to be recognized.

6

Growth of Violence

ITALY'S POSTWAR PROBLEMS worsened. Labor strikes disrupted production. Riots broke out everywhere. The government seemed helpless. The army, called out repeatedly to quell riots, became the hated arm of government. Violence was answered with violence.

On the front page of *Il Popolo d'Italia*, Mussolini replaced "The Socialist Daily" subhead with "Journal of the Fighters and Producers." He declared that fascism was the workingman's friend and had already done far more for labor than Socialists had ever dreamed of doing.

This infuriated the Socialists, but they had other problems. Because of their association with the much-feared communism, Socialists throughout Europe were on the defensive. Even the moderate Socialists could not rid themselves of communism's revolutionary taint. Thus, in a war of words, Socialists in the postwar era were vulnerable. In a war of fists and clubs, however, they could give as good as they got.

The first major street battle erupted in Milan on April 15, 1919, when a Socialist marching band met a gang of Fascists. Brass instruments were poor defense against clubs. The band was routed, and the Fascists, spurred by success, charged through the offices of *Avanti*, overturning furniture and smashing equipment. The army arrived, and before peace could be restored, one soldier was killed.

Socialists throughout Italy armed themselves for revenge. They took it first in Florence, where a gang captured and brutally murdered a young Fascist. As battle cries sounded on both sides, an unofficial war began.

The promise of violence attracted new recruits to fascism. Most were thugs who cared more for excitement than their country's future. They had little idea what the fight was about, but Mussolini welcomed them. He also welcomed cash donations from Italian businessmen and property owners who believed Mussolini was more effective than the government in the fight against communism.

The Fascists enjoyed moral and sometimes physical support from the police. Traditionally conservative, police at all levels often encouraged them. When breaking up riots, the police would often jail the Socialists and let the Fascists go.

The Fascists, however, did not have a completely free hand. Most Italians, nonviolent by nature, were shocked at the bloodshed. The Church, although opposed to communism, was also opposed to violence. Acting not so far behind the scenes, the Church encouraged creation of a moderate political party.

Don Luigi Sturzo, the Sicilian priest who organized and headed the Italian Popular Party, wanted many of the progressive reforms Mussolini had been urging, but he wanted them without the use of violence. Although Catholics were officially barred from politics, Sturzo obtained special consent from the Vatican to lead the new party. Catholics joined by the thousands. Overnight, it seemed, Sturzo had won the strength to challenge Mussolini.

In the fall elections of 1919, Sturzo's party won 101 of a total 528 seats in the Chamber of Deputies. Unfortunately, his victory undermined support for liberals who had held the majority. The Socialists' 156 seats gave them control of the Chamber.

In Milan Sturzo's party drew support away from Mussolini.

In his campaign there for the Chamber, Il Duce collected a mere 4,064 votes against 180,000 cast for the successful Socialist candidate.

A humiliated Mussolini attacked Don Sturzo and the Popular party with venomous editorials. Sturzo's counterattack was scathingly accurate.

Mussolini's mind, Sturzo wrote, "is given to excessive simplification, is bound by no formula. . . . Hence his speeches are always attuned to the state of mind of the public to which he is speaking. . . . His friends and companions he holds in esteem so long as they are useful to him . . . he abandons them to their fate when they are in his way."

Had the battle of words continued, Don Sturzo probably would have emerged the champion, but Mussolini was saved by an event that diverted attention from the contest. The event gave fascism a tremendous boost and turned it from a loose-knit collection of gangs into a military organization.

THE SURPRISE OCCUPATION of Fiume defied international treaties. The port city, well within the boundaries of the newly created Yugoslavia, had been the center of unrest since the end of the war. Fiume's large population of Italians, still hoping for annexation to Italy, kept the city in turmoil with demonstrations, strikes, and riots. To protect lives and property, an international force of American, French, British, and Italian troops had occupied Fiume. Tempers cooled, but just when it seemed that peace had been restored, an army of one thousand veterans, led by an Italian patriot, occupied the city and demanded annexation.

The campaign was headed by Gabriele d'Annunzio, a fifty-seven-year-old poet, novelist, and orator. He actually led his free booters into Fiume on September 12, 1919, several days before the fall elections, but the significance of the event was only gradually realized. Once his unofficial army controlled transportation and occupied all the government buildings, it seemed that nothing short of a siege would remove him.

The idea for d'Annunzio's campaign had come, of course, from Mussolini, who had long urged the occupation in his speeches and editorials. d'Annunzio now expected Mussolini's full support, but Il Duce had good reason to be cautious.

The mustachioed d'Annunzio, complete with monocle and a colorful uniform that included a black shirt and a black fez with tassel, was an egotistical exhibitionist. When he was writing, he ordered the church bells to ring each time he completed a poem. Thirty-five fierce watchdogs guarded his lavishly furnished home. He loved to lead parades and speak to his cheering followers. He was pompous, loud, flowery, and patriotic to the point of tears, but his men worshipped him. He had, after all, won honors for his bravery as a pilot in the war, and he championed the rights of veterans.

Once in control of Fiume, he named himself regent, appointed a legislative body, organized raids into the surrounding countryside, captured ships in or near the port, and annexed some small islands off the coast. His men, soon known as the Legionnaires, paraded daily to the town square to listen to another of his patriotic orations. Each speech was followed by organized cheers for the people of Fiume and for Gabriele d'Annunzio.

D'Annunzio had given Mussolini advance knowledge of the Fiume campaign, but Il Duce did not back it until the Legionnaires had full control of the city. Mussolini then praised the campaign and declared its leader a hero, but Il Duce never gave the Fiume campaign his full support.

He remembered the lesson of the general strike. He did not want to be associated with failure again, and he believed that the Fiume adventure, despite its romantic and symbolic appeal, would eventually fail. Mussolini also felt threatened by D'Annunzio. If the man kept getting heroic headlines he might replace Mussolini as fascism's leader.

Meanwhile, d'Annunzio aided fascism immensely. By defying his own government and its army and navy, not to mention the forces of foreign nations, he was undermining authority with greater success than Mussolini had ever dreamed. Il Duce's defiant words paled beside d'Annunzio's defiant act.

Fiume provided a showcase for fascism. d'Annunzio's black fez and black shirt became the standard Fascist uniform. Mussolini would also adopt the regular town square gatherings with speeches appealing to Italian nationalism and organized cheering.

D'Annunzio was the first to force castor oil down his enemies' throats. The castor-oil bottle was to become a favorite Fascist weapon. A large dose could and often did cause a fatal case of diarrhea.

The Fiume venture turned into a waiting game. Time was on the government's side. By raiding ships and seaports, d'Annunzio had contributed to his own downfall. Fear of his freebooters froze commerce. Supplies of food and other vital goods fell dangerously low. The city's economy came to a standstill. Faced with starvation, the citizens of Fiume, including many Italian nationals, turned against d'Annunzio.

As the months passed, ambassadors from Yugoslavia and Italy, without consulting d'Annunzio, began working on a solution. An agreement, signed by representatives of both countries in November 1920, declared Fiume an independent city and granted Italy four off-shore islands.

Mussolini used the pact as an excuse to sever connections with d'Annunzio. After praising him for keeping the city out of Yugoslavian control, Il Duce gave him no further encouragement. d'Annunzio stubbornly held his position, but his support was ebbing away.

On Christmas morning 1920, an Italian squadron lobbed a few shells at the headquarters of the occupation force. Four days later, d'Annunzio and a handful of loyal Legionnaires left the city.

Accused of abandoning the venture, Mussolini answered that the takeover of Fiume or any other city could not be achieved without a national revolt, and the time for that revolt would come only when fascism was stronger and the army was sympathetic.

"Revolution," he said early in 1921, "will be accomplished with the army, not against the army; with arms, not without them; with trained forces, not with undisciplined mobs called together in the streets."

Realistic Fascists were relieved that their leader had not involved them in a hopeless venture. Even the government officials approved of Mussolini's position. And d'Annunzio, once out of Fiume, stopped being a threat. Mussolini manipulated him into harmless obscurity.

The Fiume Legionnaires were another matter. With little encouragement they shifted their allegiance to Mussolini, and he used them to give fascism fresh spirit, new confidence, and a loyalty more intense than that found in the army. Thanks to the Legionnaires, the *fascio* were organized into a national, Fascist militia.

THE RISE OF FASCISM may have been helped at this time by a secret deal between Mussolini and Giovanni Giolitti, the prime minister and a wily veteran of Italy's Parliament. Although Mussolini denied it, Giolitti, who headed the important Liberal Democratic party, probably promised a free hand for Fascist thugs on the condition that Mussolini would support the government pact with Yugoslavia on Fiume.

Although no proof of a deal could be found, the bloody months ahead made it clear that Fascists were almost immune to arrest. Their violent attacks ended organized communism in Italy and left the Socialist party in tatters.

Italy's economy, meanwhile, worsened. Postwar inflation undermined the value of the lire. Thousands of bills were required to buy a sack of groceries. Coal supplies gave out. Shortages and labor problems brought industrial production to a halt. In 1920 alone there were 1,881 strikes. In one general strike, workers occupied factories and tried to run them, but the men lacked the knowledge for management. The venture failed. Mussolini, who had given the workers guarded support, escaped blame for the failure.

He gave most of his attention at this time to the government's handling of an army mutiny. It began when units, scheduled for duty in Albania, refused to board the boats that were to take them across the Adriatic Sea. The soldiers arrested their officers and fought off loyal troops sent to the rescue for several hours. The fighting left many men injured on both sides.

The government, overreacting to the mutiny, decided to abandon Albania and ordered the troops already stationed there withdrawn, thereby losing one of Italy's few tangible war prizes. Mussolini accused the government of everything from cowardice to treason. Public opinion supported him. Confidence in government, already low, sagged even more. Fascism gained support.

Fascism's gains became clearly evident in the city elections in the fall of 1920 with the election of many Fascist candidates. Socialists in Bologna, smarting with defeat, staged a noisy demonstration before the newly elected city council. During the melée, one of the successful Fascist candidates was shot dead.

Fascists reacted with new violence. Squads of Blackshirts roamed the streets of all major cities, beating Socialists, destroying their party offices, and breaking up their meetings. The Socialists fought back, but they were not prepared for the intensity of the Fascist attacks, and again, the police did not protect them.

Communism was no longer a potent force in Italy, but Mussolini, with constant editorials and speeches, kept the fear of both communism and socialism very much alive.

Landowners soon saw fascism as a shield against all those

who would confiscate property. Farmers, even those with just a few acres, donated food and money to local *fascio*. Almost every town in Italy soon had its Fascist headquarters and at least one squad of young Blackshirts. Socialists, also well organized, fought Fascists on every opportunity. The bloody battles sometimes lasted for days, disrupting commerce, public transportation, the mail, and other community services. Peaceful citizens grew impatient with the government's inability to restore order.

Mussolini found himself trying to balance two political extremes. Peace-loving Italians wanted the violence stopped. Mussolini supported this sentiment in editorials. On the other hand, his Blackshirts, just beginning to feel their strength, promised more violence. Mussolini gave them his support. Meanwhile, liberal elements in his party objected to the ever-growing support from industrialists and landowners. That Mussolini could hold the loyalty of all factions speaks well for his talent at doubletalk. Machiavelli would have approved.

As national elections drew near, Giolitti made the mistake of trusting Mussolini. The prime minister offered Il Duce a deal. Giolitti would let the Fascist candidates share the same ticket with Liberal Democratic candidates if Mussolini would help give Giolitti majority control of the new Parliament.

Mussolini agreed at once. The move would not only undermine support for the Socialists and for Sturzo's Popular party, but it would also give fascism the credibility it had long lacked. Joining the Liberal Democrats was like marrying into the aristocracy.

Mussolini campaigned with all his vigor. Unfortunately, he could not control his Blackshirts. Their violent attacks on Socialists continued right up to the elections, causing a damaging anti-Fascist vote. The result was that Giolitti did not receive the majority he expected.

Giolitti's party won just 159 seats in the Chamber of Deputies against 146 for the Socialists and 104 for the Popular party. Meanwhile, the Fascists won 35 seats, a substantial gain. Mussolini was elected to Parliament with a hefty 124,918 votes, far more than the 4,064 he had received in a losing effort two years earlier.

Already disheartened by the election results, Giolitti soon discovered that Mussolini had no intention of keeping any pre-election promises. On major issues, Il Duce, more often than not, aligned the Fascist members against rather than with the Liberal Democrats. The setback ended Giolitti's political career.

7

Growth of Power

MUSSOLINI APPROACHED PARLIAMENT, an institution he had often opposed, with caution. He did not fully understand the system. He was not even sure he could control his own deputies.

To his dismay, the Fascist block split on the first vote of the new Parliament. At issue was the king's traditional speech at the opening session. Mussolini said Fascists were anti-monarchy and should not invite the king to speak, but when it came to a vote, only fourteen Fascists voted with Il Duce. The king spoke.

Although Mussolini wanted to begin with a low profile, his first speech before the Chamber signaled a surprising change in party policy. He declared that fascism was not against the Church, and that it was necessary for the well-being of Italy to heal the rift between the Vatican and the government.

Despite Mussolini's consistent opposition to organized religion in any form, he now apparently realized that he could never succeed in politics while the Church opposed him.

Meanwhile, as soon as Giolitti realized the Fascists would not support him, he resigned as prime minister. The king picked Ivanhoe Bonomi, a moderate Socialist, to head the government. Fascists and Socialists now confronted each other in Parliament as well as on the streets. As a consequence street violence increased. Both sides suffered heavy losses. One battle left sixteen Fascists dead and thirty wounded.

Bonomi's government could not restore order. Soldiers and the police were demoralized or openly sympathetic with the Fascists. The average citizen, however, was fed up. One never knew from day to day if the streets would be safe, if the trains would run, if there would be food in the stores.

Alert to the public's growing impatience, Mussolini called for moderation. On June 21, 1921, he offered to disarm his Fascists if the Socialists would do likewise. This encouraged Bonomi to ask for a truce. Mussolini backed the prime minister, and despite howls from his Blackshirts, a truce was hammered out and signed by representatives of both sides.

Il Duce, however, had misjudged the depth of feeling in his own party. The Blackshirts almost to a man wanted to break the Socialist hold on labor unions, put Fascists in charge of the workers, and then take over the government. If this required violence, then violence there would be. Mussolini faced a revolt in his own party. On August 16 the Blackshirts met at Bologna and voted to condemn the truce.

Mussolini reacted at once by resigning from his party's executive committee. "The matter is settled," he wrote. "The man who is defeated must go. And I leave the top rank. I remain, and I hope I may remain, an ordinary private soldier in the Milan *fascio.*"

He hoped time would cool tempers. Meanwhile, he argued for moderation in the pages of *Il Popolo d'Italia.* Of course, he did not really expect to be "an ordinary private soldier."

The Fascist council met in Florence later in August without Mussolini, but his presence was felt. Council members, hoping to persuade Il Duce's return, postponed discussion of the controversial truce.

Before the party crisis could be resolved, Mussolini faced another from Socialist Francesco Ciccotti, who challenged him

to a duel after the editor described him in *Il Popolo d'Italia* as
"the most shameless character at large in Rome."

The two faced each other with swords at a villa in Leghorn
(Livorno), not far from Pisa. Despite fourteen assaults with
swinging blades, no blood flowed, and Ciccotti's doctors eventually stopped the contest, saying their patient's heart was too
weak for further stress. When Mussolini left the villa unscathed,
the people of Leghorn cheered him heartily.

Meanwhile, the Socialist party was having its own troubles.
At a national convention in October, the revolutionary faction
took over and pushed through a resolution condemning the
truce with Fascists that moderate Socialists had endorsed just
a few months earlier. Thus the truce was nullified without any
further strain on the Fascist party, and Mussolini, after blaming
Socialists for inviting more violence, quietly resumed leadership
of his party.

Fascists were so elated over Il Duce's return that those
attending a party conference agreed to establish fascism as an
official parliamentary party. It was a technical matter, but most
Blackshirts had previously opposed it.

A new party program, also approved at the conference,
moved the party further to the right. Among other things, the
program called for limits on government control and on the
rights of public workers to strike, an end to the demand for
eliminating the monarchy, a stronger army and navy, and a
revision of peace treaties to improve Italy's economic position.
Soon after the conference, Fascists joined other reactionaries in
Parliament to form a right-wing voting bloc.

As 1921 drew to a close, the Banca di Sconto, one of Italy's
biggest banks, failed. Thousands of small businessmen and
farmers lost their savings. The government could do nothing.
Bonomi resigned as prime minister and was replaced by Luigi
Facta, who did nothing. Confidence in the government suffered
further decline. Fascists paraded in the streets calling for the
creation of a military dictatorship.

In northern Italy, the Blackshirts had established their own military lines of command. Various districts were commanded by tough, uncompromising leaders. The most active and by far the most troublesome was Italio Balbo, who ruled the Bologna district.

Large, colorful, and fiercely independent, the twenty-five-year-old Balbo had won fame as a war pilot. He radiated vitality and confidence. He was ambitious, and he could also be cruel.

Early in 1922, in his first independent action, Balbo won the release of some jailed Fascists by threatening to kidnap the minister of agriculture who was then visiting Bologna.

Next, he organized a massive demonstration in Ferrara to demand more public works projects in the district. The demonstration turned into a military occupation. A total of sixty-three thousand armed Fascists camped in the city. Schools became military barracks, public transportation stopped, and shops, hotels, and restaurants closed their doors. Balbo was ready to occupy all Ferrara's public buildings when the government gave in and promised more employment in Balbo's district.

Mussolini was embarrassed. His fellow deputies in Parliament expected him to control Balbo. It was impossible. Mussolini could not even criticize the man publicly without rousing the anger of the Blackshirts.

Fortunately for his self-esteem, Mussolini was pleasantly distracted by foreign affairs. Early in 1922, as a correspondent for his paper, he attended the Socialist International Conference in Cannes, France, where he met politicians and correspondents from several other countries. He was treated with respect and impressed most of the people he met favorably. Later, he went to Berlin where he enjoyed a similar experience.

Luckily for Mussolini, Balbo's next campaign fizzled. He and twenty thousand Fascist militia tried to take control of Bologna itself, but city police, backed by the army, put up strong resistance. Mussolini, anxious to avoid conflict with the army, wrote Balbo:

"Dear friend, it is necessary to terminate, for a period which will be very short, your magnificent action. The state has resolved . . . for the first time . . . to resist. A pause is necessary. We must not exhaust our superb militia. I am sure you will obey my order with the same discipline you showed in your mobilization."

Balbo immediately retreated, but of course he blamed Mussolini for the humiliation. In July 1922 Balbo and his militia occupied Ravenna on the Adriatic coast. He captured the Republican headquarters and threatened to burn the building if the Republicans did not cut off Socialist association.

Not wishing to alienate his Republican colleagues in the Chamber, Mussolini ordered Balbo to suspend operations until a compromise could be arranged. Balbo was furious but complied, and Fascist and Republican politicians worked out an accord. Angry Blackshirts torched Socialist headquarters, but they left Ravenna without harming the Republicans.

Balbo next led his Blackshirts westward to Parma where he established military headquarters. Socialist militia, who were already in the city, put up a fight. The bloodshed began August 3, 1922. Balbo called at once for reinforcements, and from throughout northern Italy Blackshirts flocked to Parma. First they captured the railroad station and most school buildings. Then they gained control of the major roads leading into the city.

Within Parma, the Socialists blocked streets and put gunners on strategic rooftops. Army troops removed some street blockades, but they could not disarm the Socialists. Heavy fighting erupted. Socialists shot at Fascists and the army. Fascists shot at Socialists and the army.

From Rome, Mussolini ordered that fighting with the army be avoided at all costs. Balbo wired back that Il Duce's order came too late. Meanwhile, the Fascists slowly withdrew from the city's center, destroying Socialist property as they went. Balbo, with the city surrounded, ordered authorities to place Parma under army control. The authorities agreed and the army moved in, forcing Socialists to give up their strategic positions. Finally, Balbo led his Blackshirts in a parade through Parma's main square. It was a grand victory.

By end of summer 1922, thanks to Balbo and other district leaders, armed resistance by the Socialists was ebbing away. The district leaders had taken the risks, but Mussolini won most of the credit. Although his caution upset the Blackshirts, it won respect from many government officials. He even gained the attention of some high-ranking army officers.

MEANWHILE, HE CONTINUED to seek approval from the Church. When Pius IX was installed as the new pope, Mussolini hailed the selection in speeches and editorials, saying that a new era of improved relations between the government and the Vatican had dawned.

During this period he moved closer to the political right. He declared in one editorial that the age of democracy was dead. Political power from now on would be held by the strong and the wealthy. His liberal friends were shocked. This could not be the same revolutionary Socialist they once had known.

The government continued in turmoil. Luigi Facta, who had never been effective, had resigned as prime minister in July of 1922, but no one else wanted the job. Most parties, including the Fascists, would not actively support the formation of a new government.

Facta was persuaded to stay on temporarily. This angered the Socialists, who reacted by calling a general strike. Although weakened as a fighting force, the strike proved that the Socialists still controlled the labor unions. The country came to a standstill.

Deftly turning the situation to his advantage, Mussolini demanded that the government take immediate action against public servants who had joined the strike. When Facta failed to act, Mussolini ordered his Blackshirts to take over the vital jobs and keep public services operating. Il Duce's prompt action broke the strike and brought cheers from the public.

Even Fascist violence was condoned. When Blackshirts again burned down the Milan office of *Avanti* and then entered the city hall to chase Socialist officials from their desks, there was no public protest.

Party enrollment soared. By the end of 1922 more than one million Italians called themselves Fascists. More than two-hundred thousand were militiamen.

Workers, frustrated at last by Socialist inaction, joined Fascist unions, or national syndicates, as they were called. To the average citizen it now seemed that the Fascists were the only people in Italy who knew what to do.

Balbo and other commanders had been talking of a march on Rome, to capture control of the government, but Mussolini, although he liked the drama of the plan, advised caution. If the march failed, his ambitions might never be realized. The Blackshirts, however, were impatient and restless for action. Privately, he told them that the time for a Fascist takeover was just a few weeks away, but there was much to be done in those few weeks. It was vital to wait. Publicly, he continued to support the parliamentary system.

He refused, however, to include the Fascists in any cooperative effort with other parties to form a new government. This kept Italy in turmoil. It was exactly what Mussolini wanted.

8

The March on Rome

IN A MILD SPEECH on September 20, 1922, Mussolini told an audience that the Fascists intended to take over the government. He said violence was sometimes needed to cure bad situations, but violence without discipline or reason was a bad thing and must be controlled. Democracy had not worked in Italy. Mass rule was more often wrong than right. The tradition of monarchy was too strong for Italy to prosper without it.

Fascism would make few changes, he promised. It would simply eliminate unworkable party politics. In the new state, fascism would not represent a party; it would represent the nation.

Mussolini's quiet tone, combined with an apparent support of general elections scheduled a few weeks away, quieted the fears of his opponents. He had more difficulty keeping his Blackshirts in check. Balbo and other commanders were already organizing the march on Rome. Mussolini saw the danger of a march taking place without him.

When he tried to speak to a crowd of Blackshirts on October 11, they drowned out his voice by chanting: "To Rome! To Rome! To Rome!" He glared at them with his dark eyes and raised his arms for silence. Finally, he was able to continue his talk, but he knew the time for action had arrived.

On October 16 he met secretly with the commanders in

Milan to plan the march. It was agreed to divide leadership among three men—Cesare Maria de Vecchi, a Fascist deputy in Parliament, General Emilio de Bono, recently retired from the regular army, and Balbo. These three, along with Michele Bianchi, secretary of the Fascist party, would constitute a governing quadrumvirate to take charge of the country.

It was significant that Mussolini himself took no title. If the march should fail, he wanted others to take the blame.

The planners chose three rally centers within a twenty-five-mile radius of Rome. Here militiamen would gather to begin advancing on the capital. Civitavecchia lay on the western rail line leading from the northern provinces into Rome. Monterotondo lay on the central rail line from the north. Tivoli, twenty-two miles to the east, was the source of all water and power for Rome. It was also decided to establish a reserve center at Foligno, seventy-five miles north of Rome, and to locate headquarters for the entire operation still farther north, at Perugia. Mussolini, remaining in Milan, would be about as far from the action as he could be without leaving Italy.

When the planning session adjourned, the only major decision left was the date.

Meanwhile, rumors prompted the army to ready the defense of Rome, but Luigi Facta, still serving reluctantly and rather ignorantly as prime minister, assured everyone, including the king, that there was no cause for alarm.

Mussolini probably would have accepted peaceful transition of government to the Fascists, but he knew it was not likely to happen without some show of force. Just the same, he kept his parliamentary contacts open for negotiation. Parliament also promised a refuge in case the march should fail. As it turned out, Mussolini's parliamentary activity gave Facta and others a false feeling of security.

On the morning of October 24, however, speaking to Fascists gathered at Naples, Mussolini said an armed uprising was the party's only recourse. On the afternoon of the same day, forty thousand Fascist militia marched through the city. Although Il Duce's speech and the display of military might were both reported in Rome, Facta did nothing.

After the Naples convention Mussolini and his commanders agreed that the militia would mobilize on Friday, October 27. The march, scheduled in two phases, would start early the following day.

In the first phase, to begin at dawn on the twenty-eighth, local militias would take control of as many cities and towns as possible. In each community, city halls, police stations, post offices, radio stations, newspapers, and Socialist labor union offices would be occupied. In case of strong resistance, the militia was to avoid confrontation but do everything possible to isolate the town from other communities.

In the second phase, to start as soon as the cities and towns were occupied, all available men would be dispatched to their assigned attack centers and wait for orders to head for Rome.

It looked good on paper. The trouble was that the Blackshirts were not well enough trained or experienced to handle such a large-scale operation. With the exception of some of Balbo's ambitious ventures, most militia campaigns had been conducted independently and on a small scale.

To complicate the problem, the march on Rome would count on men who lacked battle experience of any kind. They had plenty of enthusiasm, but they did not know how to forage for themselves, and they were desperately lacking in equipment and arms. Some owned no other weapon but an old knife or a hayfork. The few who owned hunting rifles usually did not have enough ammunition to fill a coat pocket.

In Ferrara a few hours before the march, one squad in its search for weapons broke into a cavalry museum and stripped the showrooms of guns. It turned out, however, that only a few guns were still in firing order. Later, the same squad had better luck in a night raid on an armory of the regular army. They escaped with twenty muskets and six revolvers.

No matter how he were armed, each man had to provide his own clothing, bedding, and food. Even transportation was left to individual effort and ingenuity.

On the day of mobilization, roads soon became crowded with old trucks, farm carts, and horse carriages, all loaded to capacity with ragtag militia. Trains were jammed with noisy crowds. The regular commuters stared in disbelief at Blackshirts "armed" with farm hoes, table legs, and tree roots. One man carried a golf club. Another had sticks of dynamite hanging from his belt.

During most of that Friday morning, a carnival spirit filled the clear autumn air. In the afternoon, however, clouds began to gather. By nightfall, a cold rain lashed northern Italy. The tired men found shelter in barns, vineyard sheds, old kilns, abandoned villas, and wine cellars. Some, with great distance to cover, kept traveling through the night. The temperature dropped below freezing. Mussolini's "army" was almost beaten by the elements before the campaign began.

Saturday morning there were only four thousand Blackshirts at Tivoli, one thousand three hundred at Monterotondo, and an uncertain number at Civitavecchia. Although forces at the attack points grew during the morning as others straggled in, no one knew what to do next. They were supposed to wait for orders, but little had been done to arrange communication between the attack centers and campaign headquarters at Perugia.

Headquarters itself, in Perugia's Hotel Brufani, was torn with confusion. de Vecchi and Bianchi, two members of the quadrumvirate, were not even there. They were in Rome where de Vecchi was still trying to negotiate a parliamentary settlement and Bianchi was doing his best to prevent it.

There were many rumors and little news. One false report had it that Facta had resigned, leaving the way open for a peaceful Fascist takeover. Thinking that the march might not be necessary, the Fascist commanders delayed issuing orders. Several isolated commanders, however, not accustomed to orders of any kind, led their men down the road to Rome.

There were a few scrimmages with government troops. The bloodiest of these occurred at Cremona, in northern Italy, where army guards fired on the militia, killing seven Blackshirts. Meanwhile, closer to Rome, army troops began tearing up railroad tracks to slow the march.

The Italian army, well equipped and well led, could easily have routed the poorly organized Fascists. But the army lacked one vital thing—an order. Neither the king nor Facta was willing to take responsibility, and the two men disliked each other too much to act together.

The king, in fact, had already begun to regard the Fascists more as a solution than a threat. Mussolini had, after all, promised to preserve the monarchy. Facta had done nothing and promised nothing.

The animosity between king and prime minister came to a head on the Saturday morning after an all-night meeting of Cabinet ministers. The Cabinet first instructed Facta to tell the army to "use all possible means to maintain public order and security." Facta did this without consulting the king. Next, the Cabinet drafted a royal proclamation declaring war on the Fascists and told Facta to take it to the king.

At the palace, the king was so angry about not being consulted that he snatched the proclamation out of Facta's hand, glanced at it, and then slammed it into a desk drawer.

Facta hurried away in confusion. He issued an order canceling the earlier instructions for the army to resist the Fascists. The result of all this was to leave the roads to Rome undefended and a proclamation of war unsigned.

The king, meanwhile, made a final effort to form a new government that would negotiate with Mussolini. He asked Antonio Salandra, a former prime minister, to meet de Vecchi, who was still in Rome, and Costanzo Ciano, an emissary Mussolini had sent from Milan. Salandra proposed a government that would give Mussolini a dominant role in the Cabinet. Ciano and de Vecchi approved the proposal, but when they telephoned Mussolini in Milan, he turned the plan down.

While these desperate negotiations were in progress, the ragtag marchers gradually discovered that no one stood in their way. The march turned into a triumphant parade. Some units, however, waiting for orders that never came, failed to join the parade.

In the offices of *Il Popolo d'Italia* in Milan, Mussolini suspected that Facta's order for the army not to resist was a trap. Later, when word of the king's willingness to trust Mussolini with the formation of a new government reached Milan, he was again suspicious. He demanded and got confirmation by government cable. The historic message said:

> "His Majesty the King begs you to proceed to Rome as soon as possible as he wishes to entrust you with the task of forming a cabinet."

Mussolini grinned with satisfaction. He had won. The government of Italy was his at last.

There were two last-minute tasks remaining in Milan. The first was easy. He ordered the destruction of the offices of *Avanti.* This would prevent the Socialists from organizing a general strike or any other resistance.

The second job took more time. He wanted to put out a special edition of his own paper to announce his triumph. His final editorial concluded:

> "Fascism will not abuse its victory, but is determined that it shall not be diminished. Let that be clear to all. Nothing shall disturb the beauty and the ardor of our offensive. The Fascists have been and are admirable. Their self-sacrifice is great and must be crowned by complete victory. Any other solution is to be rejected."

At last he was ready. At 8:30 P.M., Sunday, October 29, 1922, he boarded the train for Rome.

At each station, Italians on both sides of the tracks cheered him. He got out of his first-class coach at Piacenza, Pisa, Carrara, and Civitavecchia to review proud ranks of militiamen who had taken no more part in the march than Mussolini himself.

Although he had not marched, many sleepless nights and the excitement of the journey had left him pale and tired. When he stepped from the train in Rome, he did not look impressive. He wore a black shirt, a wrinkled morning coat, black trousers, and a bowler hat. His shabby shoes were hidden under spats that had been dusted with talcum powder to hide the stains. His serious face was almost as white as the spats.

Mussolini went directly to the royal palace. At 11:45 A.M., Monday, October 30, he strode into the royal chamber. Although stiff and awkward, he had his opening line well rehearsed. He shook the king's hand and said:

"Your majesty will forgive my attire—I have come from the battlefield."

Young Mussolini put on formal attire for this 1904 photo taken in Switzerland. As a revolutionary Socialist, he was not noted at the time for stylish clothes. [UPI/Bettmann News Photos]

Rachele Mussolini [National Archives]

At the beginning of World War I, when Mussolini was urging Italy to give up neutrality, the large brow and piercing eyes had become the dominant features of his face. The mustache was shaved off soon after the war. [UPI/Bettmann News Photos]

Mussolini, wearing a white ribbon and spats, joined the October 1922 "March on Rome" in time to have his photo taken with other leaders of the Fascist takeover. [New York Public Library]

The prime minister in a top hat stands on the reviewing stand with Italo Balbo, vice minister of the air force, for a 1927 air show near Rome. Balbo was killed in World War II when his plane was shot down in Libya. [UPI/Bettmann News Photos]

Mussolini pitches hay to promote increased farm production during one of the Fascist government's many carefully planned publicity campaigns. Though the campaigns did not always achieve their goals, they did boost Italian pride and spirit. [UPI/Bettmann News Photos]

Bruno, Vittorio, Edda, and Ciano (left to right) are the center of attention as the three men prepare to sail from Naples for the campaign in Abyssinia in September 1935. The three, all air force officers, soon returned to Italy, but only Vittorio would survive the Fascist regime. [UPI/Bettmann News Photos]

The balcony of the Palazzo Venezia was Mussolini's favorite platform. Here he could address his Roman fans and glory in their cheers. [National Archives]

Mussolini's jutting chin and broad brow, which he accented by shaving his scalp, became features that were mocked and characterized by western writers and cartoonists during World War II. [National Archives]

9

The Prime Minister

THE MOMENT THE KING named him prime minister, Mussolini no longer needed his ragtag army, but he wanted the march completed. It would not only satisfy the Blackshirts' need for heroics, but it would also give his new regime dramatic endorsement. The appearance in Rome of the tired but happy "army" did indeed accent the national emotions of the hour.

He rode into office on a wave of popularity. There had been three years of bloodshed. The fighting between Socialists and Fascists had been a civil war in everything but name. Now there was hope of peace at last.

Even the king, who received hundreds of telegrams congratulating him for naming Mussolini, was enthusiastic.

"He really is a man of purpose," the king told an aide, "and I can tell you that he will last some time. There is in him, if I am not mistaken, the will to act and act well. When I told him to put together an administration on a broad basis and with capable men, I felt that he agreed and was close to my views. I had previously formed quite a different impression of him."

It was now up to Mussolini to prepare a list of ministers to be appointed to his cabinet. Of the fourteen he selected, ten were already members of Parliament. Only four candidates for the ministry were Fascists. The others gave a balanced representation for other parties. Just half of the undersecretary appointees were Fascists.

He said he avoided an all-Fascist cabinet because he wanted to give the country a broad base and the promise of normal politics, but the truth was that very few Fascists had the experience for political office. Mussolini appointed himself minister of both the Department of Interior and the Department of Foreign Affairs largely because he could find no one else qualified for the positions.

Many party leaders were keenly disappointed. de Vecchi was the only member of the quadrumvirate to win a job, and that was the minor post of undersecretary for military pensions. All complaints, however, were muffled under Il Duce's popularity.

When he and the king appeared together on a palace balcony, the cheering was like thunder. It continued as the king stepped into his office to put the royal seal on Mussolini's list of cabinet ministers.

Mussolini was exhausted, but before resting, he organized transportation to take his Blackshirts home. It was a difficult job. Buses and trains had to be rescheduled and rerouted, but finally the last trainload of militiamen pulled out of Rome on the evening of October 31. The city returned to normal. The new prime minister of Italy went to bed.

He was only thirty-nine years old, making him the youngest of all the twenty-four previous Italian prime ministers. He was also perhaps the most mysterious man to come to the office. Outside of Milan and Forli, the two cities where he was well known, Mussolini was little more than a name to most Italians. His Fascists had been in existence just four years. He had been a member of Parliament for no more than a year and a half.

He made a good first impression. He could be modest, sincere, and very courteous. He presented the picture of a young man well aware of the difficulties before him but courageous and resolved enough to meet the difficulties head on.

Although stocky and short, he gave the impression of being

a taller man. He had a massive jaw and a brow made large by a receding hairline. But his eyes dominated his face. They were dark, intense, and large, and he had the habit of raising his lids to emphasize a point. His eyes, it seems, made him irresistible to some women.

In public, he lost his easy charm and struck a pose—back stiff, hands on hips, chin thrust out. It seemed to be his idea of how a Roman emperor should look. It made him appear to be a man of iron. That was the effect he wanted.

Behind the public pose, however, he lacked confidence. Decisions, at first, were very difficult for him. A career in journalism had not prepared him for the detailed work of government administration.

Fortunately, most Italians were willing to give the new man a chance, and Mussolini was a quick learner. He had an uncanny ability to catch the core of a problem in just a few moments of conversation or just a brief glance at a report. He was an avid and rapid reader. He went through a stack of newspapers daily; they were a major interest. He also paid close attention to reports from his secret service. He was particularly fascinated with descriptions of the private lives of government officials. As the years passed, he put more and more importance on these reports. Even though much information was founded on rumor and hearsay, Mussolini decided from the reports who was friendly and who was unfriendly to his regime. Often he acted on these reports without further investigation. Abrupt, unexplained dismissals became a trademark of the Fascist regime.

In the early days, however, his main interest was to give the public an image of a confident but moderate ruler, interested in reform but not willing to make radical change. To friends he admitted that he must feel his way slowly.

The first challenge to his regime came from Don Sturzo who opposed Mussolini's request for full powers to run the government. Mussolini made the request on November 22, 1922, in his first speech to Parliament as prime minister: "I do not wish to govern against the wishes of the Chamber; but the Chamber must understand the peculiar position it holds, which makes it liable to dismissal in two days or two years. We ask for full powers because we wish to take full responsibility."

The Senate and the Chamber of Deputies promptly granted Mussolini full powers, but Don Sturzo called the request political blackmail and refused to accept it quietly. Unfortunately for Sturzo, his own party split on the issue. Half his delegates wanted to back Mussolini; the other half wanted to oppose him at every opportunity. At the Popular party's annual congress, Sturzo had to adopt a platform favoring limited cooperation with Mussolini. Although the compromise saved the party, it weakened it at a time when strength was vital for political survival.

Mussolini, objecting to any party that stood for "limited" cooperation with his regime, dismissed the six Popular party members from his cabinet and launched a vicious newspaper attack on Sturzo. Under this attack, the extreme factions bolted and Sturzo resigned as party chairman. The Popular party crumbled.

Il Duce's next proposal to Parliament, a revision of election laws, passed virtually unchallenged. Under the new law, the party receiving the most votes in a general election would automatically receive a commanding two-thirds majority of the seats in Parliament. This did away with the old difficulty of forming a government when no majority existed in Parliament, and of course it put Parliament firmly in Fascist hands. Mussolini had only to avoid calling an election when a Fascist majority seemed in doubt.

The new election law, more than any change so far, brought down the curtain on Italian democracy. But the Chamber of Deputies and the Senate both voted overwhelmingly for it.

Although domestic matters were a major concern at this time, Mussolini used meetings with diplomats and ambassadors to build his image as a statesman. The meetings were usually reported at great length in the world press. And by appearing as a responsible, thoughtful, and friendly leader, Mussolini raised Italy's stature in the community of nations. It brought back some of the pride that Italians had lost in the disaster of postwar diplomacy.

Early in his first year as prime minister, Mussolini attended two foreign conferences, one at Lausanne, Switzerland, to discuss Turkish borders, and another in London, England, to discuss German war reparations. The conferences settled few problems, but Mussolini gained stature both at home and abroad by insisting that Italy be treated as an equal partner in all debates. He enjoyed heroic returns to Rome from both conferences.

His handling of his first foreign crisis left Italians cheering. The crisis arose from a border dispute between Greece and Albania. Mussolini had sent several men to represent Italy on an international commission formed to survey the dispute. All was going well until August 27, 1923, when the bodies of all the Italian members of the commission were discovered on Greek territory. They had been murdered.

In a rage, Mussolini sent the Greek government a list of harsh demands, including a public apology, immediate inquiry into the killings, the death sentence for those convicted of the crime, and the payment of fifty million lire within five days. The Greek government, not even sure that Greeks were responsible, refused to meet the demands.

Mussolini ordered the Italian navy to bombard the island of Corfu (Kerkyra) off the Greek coast. The shelling, which killed several Greek civilians, was followed by the amphibious landing of Italian marines.

When the council of the League of Nations condemned the Italian operation, Mussolini threatened to pull Italy out of the League. He insisted that the Conference of Ambassadors, the international body that had created the survey commission, must arbitrate the dispute.

The ambassadors met on September 7. Fortunately for

Italy, France and Germany were locked in struggle for control of the mineral-rich Ruhr Valley. France, wanting Italy to support its border demands in the Ruhr, sided with Italy in the Greek crisis. As a result, the Conference of Ambassadors lost little time in endorsing most of Italy's position.

The Greek government gave in and agreed to Il Duce's demands. It was a triumph of diplomacy and luck.

He followed the Greek victory with the satisfactory settlement of the Fiume dispute. Since d'Annunzio's surrender, Fiume had been an open city, belonging to no nation. The status had extended the city's economic depression. Factories remained idle. The railroad, torn up during the occupation, had never been rebuilt. Starvation was prevented only through the dole of food by the Italian government.

Mussolini opened negotiations with Yugoslavia by proposing that Italy take full possession of Fiume in exchange for some Italian border territory that would be transferred to Yugoslavia. When a joint Yugoslavian-Italian commission failed to act promptly on his proposal, Mussolini sent units of the Italian army into the city.

Yugoslavia, realizing that Fiume was now all but lost, agreed to the swap. A pact was signed by both sides on January 27, 1924. King Victor Emmanuel III was so pleased that he draped the Collar of Annunziata, Italy's highest royal honor, around Il Duce's neck.

It seemed that his popularity would continue to grow forever. But at this point Mussolini made a serious mistake. No one knows why he decided to call a general election. It was not necessary. Perhaps he had to have some solid proof of his popularity. Maybe he simply wanted to see how the new election laws would work.

The preelection campaigning revealed that despite his immense popularity, some people remained strongly opposed to his regime. His opponents included Socialists who had seen their party crushed and many individuals who had tasted Fascist castor oil or been subjected to other cruel treatment. The election gave opponents the incentive to organize. It even revitalized the Popular party.

The rise of opposition gave the Blackshirts, idle and restless since the march on Rome, a chance for more violence, and as soon as their attacks on opposition offices and candidates began, reaction loomed.

Campaigning grew heated. As usual Mussolini tried to play a double role. Publicly, he condemned the violence. Privately, he approved the activities of his Blackshirts. Publicly, he assured voters that fascism would protect the constitution and preserve civil liberties. Privately, he told militia leaders that this would be the last general election ever held in Italy.

Violence reigned unchecked right up to the eve of the April 6 election. Clearly, Mussolini could not curb it. Blackshirts murdered a Socialist candidate and assaulted a priest who had endorsed the Popular party. The violence angered peace-loving Italians and prompted a large opposition vote.

It was not large enough to overthrow the government— three million votes against some four million for Fascists. Mussolini, however, was shocked. He had not anticipated any opposition vote worth counting. Unfortunately, even after the election ended, the violence continued. Mussolini did little to stop it. In fact, in his anger, he probably encouraged it.

Inevitably, the violence led to a national crisis. It began on June 10, barely two months after the elections, when Giacomo Matteotti, a popular Socialist member of the Chamber of Deputies, was reported missing.

10

The Matteotti Case

GIACOMO MATTEOTTI, thirty-nine years old and full of energy, was fascism's loudest and most effective opponent. He campaigned vigorously for Socialists before the election, and when it was over, he rose in Parliament to challenge the validity of the voting and demand restoration of the old voting laws. He used his anger and cutting sarcasm to put the Fascists on the defensive.

The Fascist deputies tried to smother Matteotti's speech with hoots and shouts, but this only focused attention on the young Socialist's words. Other opposition voices soon joined Matteotti in the attack on the government. He was fearless. In one noisy session, Matteotti and Mussolini shouted accusations at each other. Matteotti did not give an inch to the prime minister. In fact, it was Mussolini who seemed to lose control. In a rage, he shook his fist at the Socialist and shouted, "You should receive a charge of lead in the back!"

Matteotti did not blink, but Il Duce's ill-chosen words were soon to haunt him.

On June 11, 1924, a week after the shouting match, Matteotti was reported missing. The Fascists were suspected at once. Mussolini, facing a storm of public outcry, was put on the defensive, never his best position. On June 12 Il Duce told the

Chamber of Deputies that all government resources were being used to find out what had happened.

Indeed, the police did make progress, and it soon became certain that Fascists were responsible for the deputy's disappearance.

On the morning of June 13, all the non-Fascist deputies marched out of Parliament promising not to return until the case was solved and everyone responsible was brought to justice. This proved to be a costly political mistake. The case was not solved for a long, long time, and by being absent, the opposition lost its voice in Italy's destiny.

THE INVESTIGATION led to three men. Amerigo Dumini, a war veteran and Fascist activist, worked as an undercover investigator for the government press department. Cesare Rossi, head of the press department, had once served on the staff of *Il Popolo d'Italia*. Giovanni Marinelli, who had left the Socialist party with Mussolini, had become treasurer of the Fascist party. Directly or indirectly, Mussolini had requested these three to investigate anti-Fascist activities.

Dumini had been commissioned to keep an eye on Matteotti. Driving a large borrowed car, Dumini followed the Socialist deputy and became familiar with his habits. After several days of this, he enlisted a driver and four Fascist thugs. The plan was to kidnap Matteotti and try to frighten him into silence. To this day, no one can be sure where the plan originated.

On the afternoon of June 10, Dumini and the driver waited in the car outside Matteotti's home while the thugs waited on the sidewalk. When the Socialist emerged from his home to head for the evening session of Parliament, the thugs seized him and after a short struggle forced him into the car, which then sped away.

There were two witnesses, a street cleaner and a lawyer. They gave police the license number of the car, which was then traced to the criminals. In a few days, Dumini and four other men were arrested. Later, the fifth, who had fled to France, was captured and brought back to Rome. All denied any part in the crime, and because no body had yet been found, police were stymied. But then Filippo Filippelli told his story. He was the owner of the car.

He told police he had lent it with the understanding that Dumini planned to show some visitors the sights of Rome. Filippelli stated that Dumini returned late on June 10 in great agitation. Dumini spoke of a "sad bungle." He said Matteotti was dead.

Filippelli, who apparently knew nothing of the plot, demanded an explanation. Dumini said he had acted for Mussolini on instructions relayed by Marinelli and Rossi. The plan had been to teach Matteotti a lesson by abducting him on his way to Parliament, but the deputy had struggled in the backseat of the car and been killed by a stab wound.

The car was so badly stained with blood that it would be necessary to dispose of it. Filippelli agreed to hide the car overnight with the understanding that Dumini and his thugs would get rid of it the next morning.

Filippelli's sworn statement led to the arrest of Marinelli and Rossi. Rossi, who made a full statement at once, said he helped head an undercover shock squad that Mussolini had created to intimidate opponents of fascism. Other leaders of the squad were Marinelli and Emilio de Bono, one of the commanders of the march on Rome who was now a senator and director of public security. The squad was authorized to use violence and threats of violence. They were even licensed to beat their victims, give them a dose of castor oil, and, if necessary, kill. Although Rossi denied any knowledge of the Matteotti case, he admitted that he had hired Dumini to do the squad's dirty work.

Rossi further described how three opposition members of Parliament had already been beaten by Dumini and his men. In each case, Rossi said, the beating was reported to Mussolini, who voiced pleasure at the news. Police investigators next obtained a statement from one of Dumini's thugs who said Mussolini had ordered Matteotti's murder.

Although details of the confessions were not published, rumors linking Mussolini to the crime spread throughout Italy. In just a few days, the national hero had become the national enemy. It seemed that fascism was finished.

His office in the Palazzo Venezia, once bustling with office seekers and friends, was now empty. The plaza below his window, once crowded with cheering citizens, was now the gathering place for angry groups. The people shouted threats and shook fists at him whenever he appeared in the window.

He spoke privately of resigning and asking the king to form a new government. He was on the verge of a nervous breakdown, but gradually his aggressive nature rescued him from depression.

On June 24, Mussolini spoke with tact and moderation before the Senate. He expressed horror at the crime, promised an end to all violence, and vowed to defend parliamentary government. He concluded by asking for a vote of confidence. He got it with an overwhelming 252 to 21 vote.

Mussolini suddenly realized that he faced no organized opposition.

Had the minority remained in Parliament, the situation could have been much more difficult for Il Duce. Had they remained in the Chamber, the minority deputies would have at least gained some attention from the press. As individuals outside the Chamber, however, they had no influence over public opinion and little chance to organize.

Mussolini, with all the power of government on his side, went to work. Behind the scenes, officials began pressuring investigators to slow down their inquiry. Fascists who cooperated with police were dismissed from office. Others were threatened into silence.

Much to his credit, Mauro del Giudice, president of the criminal court assigned to the case, resisted pressure from both the Fascists and their opponents. He was determined to find the truth.

Truth, however, was the last thing Mussolini wanted. In a July decree, he gave cities the power to suppress newspapers for publishing anything that might disturb the peace or incite crime and violence. The press was further prohibited from verbal attack on the king, the pope, or the government. This was Mussolini's first censorship law. It made editors cautious about printing rumors on the Matteotti case. But the facts had to come out.

On August 16 Matteotti's bruised and bloody body was found in a ditch twelve miles outside of Rome. Despite the censorship decrees, the press carried all the details. All Italy soon knew that Matteotti had been stabbed to death.

The news touched off a public outcry. Citizens everywhere demanded justice. The court process could no longer be delayed. By mid-November, with forty-four volumes of testimony at hand, del Giudice was ready to open the trial.

Although it would have risked riots, Mussolini probably was ready to stop the trial, but then a Catholic editor unwittingly came to the rescue. The editor, a dedicated foe of fascism, demanded that de Bono be tried before the Senate. Grounds for the demand were that del Giudice was a Fascist tool, and only the Senate could give a fair trial. In truth, Del Giudice was no one's tool, and the Senate, dominated by Fascists, was already on uneasy terms with justice.

But the editor was as persuasive as he was poorly informed. No one protested when Mussolini ordered the trial delayed while the case against de Bono was heard by his fellow senators.

The result was never in doubt, but the Senate deliberately took a long time on the case. As long as it was hearing the case, the Senate could hold all the evidence that del Giudice had so carefully accumulated. Without the evidence, Rossi, Marinelli,

Dumini, and his thugs could not be tried. The Senate did not hurry. Six months passed before it declared de Bono's innocence.

Mussolini, meanwhile, had further undermined the judicial process. He granted amnesty to all prisoners awaiting trial for any crimes short of murder. Next, he had del Giudice promoted to a higher court in Sicily, far from Rome, and replaced him with a judge who was willing to reduce charges in the Matteotti case.

Now, instead of a murder charge, the defendants were accused of contributing to accidental death. The reasoning was that although the abduction of Matteotti was premeditated, his death was due in part to his struggles in the backseat of the car.

The reduced charges coupled with the amnesty made it possible to release Rossi and Marinelli. Only Dumini and his thugs were left to stand trail. And when the trial finally took place, the scene was a courtroom in Chieti, a small town one hundred miles east of Rome. There, it was established that Matteotti had indeed been stabbed, but the judge allowed additional testimony that said Matteotti suffered from a disease that contributed to his death.

The verdict was that Dumini and two others, found guilty of abducting Matteotti, should each serve five years, eleven months, and twenty days in prison. A detailed provision of Il Duce's amnesty decree, however, allowed a four-year reduction of the sentence, and because credit was given for time already spent in jail, the three were released the moment the trial ended.

No evidence implicating Mussolini was introduced at the trial or again in 1947 when the case was reopened at the insistence of Matteotti's widow. In the postwar tribunal, three surviving suspects were found guilty of premeditated murder and sentenced to thirty years in prison. Thus the case, not finally closed until after Mussolini had been dead for two years, ended with some degree of justice at last.

11

The Dictator

MATTEOTTI'S MURDER marked an ominous turning point for Italy.

It destroyed the last hope for the democratic process. Mussolini had envisioned formation in Parliament of a United Socialist-Fascist party, but the Matteotti case buried the possibility forever. Now he could see no reason to keep any trace of the old system, and the opposition, by withdrawing from Parliament, had lost the chance to defend it.

The weakness of his opposition convinced Mussolini that it was not only possible but also advisable to become dictator of Italy. He began methodically gathering power.

On January 3, 1925, in the Chamber of Deputies, he attacked the opposition for abandoning the Chamber in a crisis and for trying to exploit a national tragedy. Peace had been preserved, he claimed, only because he had held the Blackshirts in check. Now things would change.

Complaints against the various branches of government, he said, would no longer be tolerated. From now on, anyone with a complaint must come to him. He would be responsible for everything because he would have power over everything.

Of course, this bold challenge was cheered by the Fascists. No one opposed it because no other party was represented in the Chamber. And Mussolini's speech echoed the mood of the country. Italians were fed up with violence, strikes, and riots. They wanted a man of strength to take charge and lead the country through its difficulties. Il Duce was ready and willing to do the job.

Luckily, Italy's economy had at last begun to improve. Poverty and unemployment slowly declined. Some regions enjoyed a mild boom. Influential Italians, busy trying to take advantage of prosperity, did not pay much attention to changes in government.

Mussolini could thus replace constitutional government with a dictatorship without much attention or criticism. His first step was to mobilize the Blackshirts as an enforcement branch of the government. They were ordered to arrest anyone suspected of anti-Fascist ideas or activities. The Blackshirts also had orders to close clubs and associations that had or might someday oppose Mussolini.

On January 6, just three days after his tough speech to Parliament, 111 individuals had been arrested, 655 homes had been searched, and 204 organizations had been closed down.

Meanwhile, the new press law, established earlier by Il Duce's decree, began to be enforced with vigor. Opposition newspapers were seized one after the other. Some were closed. Others were converted to Fascist journals. Later, in another press decree, Mussolini made it impossible for anyone who was not a member of the Fascist party to work for an Italian newspaper.

Opposition leaders made one last attempt to stop Mussolini. They appealed to the king, telling him that Il Duce was methodically destroying the constitution and should be deposed. The king refused to act. He believed that any attempt to dislodge Mussolini might lead to the loss of the monarchy itself.

Without the king's help, opponents could continue to fight and risk arrest and loss of property, or they could go underground, becoming politically inactive, and hope that Mussolini would one day lose his grip on the government. Most took the second choice, but some took a third choice. They left Italy. These expatriates risked loss of their property, but in France, Switzerland, or some other friendly country they were free to speak their minds and criticize the Fascist regime.

There was a fourth choice—a desperate and bloody one, but a few took it.

During 1925 there were four attempts on Mussolini's life. On November 4, Tito Zaniboni was accused of planning to kill Il Duce. He was sentenced to thirty years in prison. Zaniboni happened to be a Freemason and because of this, the Blackshirts were ordered to close Masonic lodges throughout Italy.

On April 26, Violet Gibson, an Englishwoman, fired a pistol at Il Duce. The bullet scratched his nose. Miss Gibson was arrested, but her motives had not been political. One of Mussolini's many ex-mistresses, she had been coldly spurned and was trying to revenge her honor with hot lead. To keep attention off the affair, Miss Gibson was simply sent back to England without trial.

On September 11, Gino Lucetti, an anarchist, tossed a bomb at Mussolini's car. Four persons were injured, but Il Duce was unscathed. Lucetti was captured immediately and sentenced to thirty years in prison.

On October 13, a shot was fired at Mussolini's car in the streets of Naples. A street crowd, suspecting fifteen-year-old Anteo Zamboni of the deed, lynched him on the spot. Later, however, it appeared that Zamboni was innocent. Some people even suspected that the "assassination" attempt may have been staged by the Blackshirts to have an excuse for tighter security.

The fact was that all incidents were used as an excuse to intensify the anti-Fascist crackdown. The castor oil flowed once again. There were brutal beatings. Giovanni Amendola, who once had opposed the Fascists in Parliament, was beaten so severely that he eventually died of his wounds.

Mussolini issued new decrees almost daily. All secret organizations were prohibited, and all other organizations were required to report their activities and give their membership lists to the government.

Another decree made it illegal for any government official to oppose Fascist policies. First to be dismissed under this law were several college professors who demanded academic freedom.

In an attempt to silence critics who had left Italy, Mussolini decreed that any Italian, whether living at home or abroad, would lose his or her property for speaking against fascism.

Additional decrees came in rapid order. Mussolini listed assassination, treason, and insurrection as crimes punishable by death. He gave himself the power to govern entirely by decree if he wished. He ruled that nothing could be discussed in Parliament without first obtaining his permission. He discontinued local elections throughout Italy, saying that henceforth city officials would be appointed and serve at his discretion.

During this period Mussolini instituted what became known as the corporate state. It put every economic activity in the country under a government-appointed panel, or "corporation." Representatives of management and labor, in each industry, served on these panels. They were to obtain sales and production contracts, settle labor disputes, and set up worker training and welfare programs. All profits under the corporate state would go to the government.

Meanwhile, Parliament became a tool of the corporate state. Candidates for the Chamber of Deputies and the Senate would be proposed by the various corporate panels. The list of candidates would then go to the grand council of the Fascist party, which would selected four hundred to serve in Parliament.

The grand council, nothing more than a committee of Mussolini henchmen, would control the functions of the Senate and Chamber, and also select successors to the throne. Privately, the king protested, but he lacked the backing to challenge Mussolini openly.

While Mussolini built his power at home, he lost prestige abroad.

In Locarno, Switzerland, during a national conference held to settle the German-French dispute over the Ruhr Valley, Mussolini scheduled a press conference in his hotel lobby. No one came. Because of Matteotti's murder, members of the international press had decided to boycott Mussolini. Later, when the delegates were gathering, the chief Belgian delegate, a Socialist, refused to shake Mussolini's hand.

When an English delegate wondered aloud before the start of one session if the Fascists would attend in black shirts, a Frenchman responded loudly that he was more curious to see if they showed up in clean shirts. The slur became the joke of the conference.

For his part, Mussolini did not try to hide his hate for France, which had given haven to many anti-Fascists. He did, however, improve his relations with England, laying the foundation for a friendship that was to last for several years.

Just the same, the Locarno conference was a disappointment and an embarrassment. Mussolini, however, did not lose interest in foreign affairs. He hoped to expand Italy's influence and perhaps its borders through diplomacy.

His persistence won dividends at his next foreign venture, this time at Tirana, Albania, where diplomats met in November of 1926. Across the Adriatic Sea from Italy, Albania was the buffer between Yugoslavia and Greece. The country had once been under Italian protection, but Italy had given up its claim during the army mutiny.

Now, at Tirana, overcoming the objections of Yugoslavia and France, Mussolini regained Albania as an Italian protectorate.

Il Duce received a hero's welcome when he returned to Rome. His dream of empire just might come true.

Meanwhile, Mussolini had begun working on the most challenging undertaking of his young regime. It was not easy, but he was determined to mend the rift between the Church and the government. To show his sincerity, he made a personal commitment by leading Rachele to a church where they were married on their knees before a priest.

The quiet wedding had taken place on Christmas Day, 1925. They already had three children: Edda, born in 1910; Vittorio, in 1915; and Bruno, born in 1923. Mussolini explained to surprised friends that he thought it was his duty as head of the government to conform to his country's religious traditions. Actually, his main reason was to smooth the way for negotiations with the Vatican.

The Black-White conflict, dating back to Italian unification in 1859, had shifted focus. Although Church lands had been reduced from 16,000 square miles to the mere 500,000 square yards of Vatican City, property was no longer the main issue. The Church was far more concerned about its authority. Such things as the right to appoint bishops, sanctify marriages, and educate children belonged to the Church only by tradition. There were no laws guaranteeing them. Even the land under Vatican City technically belonged to the government. Tradition alone allowed the Church to occupy the property.

The Church wanted a treaty, just like any treaty between two governments, to preserve its rights for all time. Otherwise it would remain at the mercy of whatever unpredictable government might be in power.

Various popes had tried to force previous governments to the treaty table. To spark some interest, Pope Pius IX, who described himself as a Vatican prisoner, laid formal claim to all Church lands that the government had earlier confiscated.

The government ignored the claim, but Leo XIII and other popes who followed took the same position, and maintained that Catholics must not participate in politics or hold government office until a treaty was signed by both sides in the dispute.

Mussolini, whose speeches and editorials had once dripped with anticlerical venom, seemed to be the least likely man to lead his government to the treaty table, but ever since his first days in politics he had been making friendly overtures to the Church. His marriage was one of many such overtures.

On May 4, 1926, in a long letter to the pope, Mussolini said that his government would welcome an accord. He invited negotiations to begin.

It took three months for the Vatican to respond, but after listing many complex conditions, it accepted the invitation to talk and a long series of secret meetings began.

Pope Pius XI was just as eager as Mussolini was for an accord. The negotiations made good progress well into the fall of 1926, but then the Blackshirts embarrassed Mussolini by attacking Church buildings in fourteen different cities. The Church pulled out of the talks at once.

Il Duce apologized publicly. He ordered the Blackshirts to leave Church property alone. After weeks of waiting, the Church finally returned to the conference table.

Progress was again being made when the Church withdrew again. Mussolini had proposed a law that would give the government full control of political and physical education and dissolve the Catholic groups that had been providing this instruction. The Vatican suspended negotiations indefinitely.

Eventually, however, Pope Pius realized that only with the treaty he was seeking would the Church be safe from the very kind of legislation Mussolini was proposing. Highly secret negotiations were thus allowed to continue. In February 1929 the treaty was ready to be signed.

It said the Church would recognize the civil rights of the Italian government. In exchange, the government would pay seven hundred and fifty million lire in cash and one billion lire in bonds as payment for the confiscated Church lands. In addition, the government would make religious education part of all elementary and secondary schools and use only those teachers and books approved by the Church. Marriages would be automatically legalized by the state, and judgments on dissolution of any marriage would be entirely up to the Church.

The government was actually giving up few rights not already belonging to the Church by tradition. Although Mussolini had wanted government control of marriage contracts, he was generally pleased with the treaty.

Representatives of both sides ratified the treaty on February 11, 1929. Now it remained only to publish the treaty and have it signed. The public reaction was everything Mussolini hoped it would be. There were parades and celebrations. Citizens cheered both the pope and Il Duce. Church officials gave generous credit to Mussolini for making the treaty a reality. In a wave of well-being and national pride, it seemed to many Italians that Mussolini's regime had been sanctioned by the Church.

The good feelings did not last. Even before the treaty was formally signed, Mussolini and the Vatican were at odds again over small issues. There was some fear that the treaty might be torn up, but at last Mussolini led a large government delegation to the Vatican, sat down at a table, and penned his name on the document.

It was a high point in his career. Indeed, his prestige was never higher.

12

The Builder

WITH NO ORGANIZED OPPOSITION to embarrass him, Mussolini confidently scheduled national elections for March 24, 1929. Although Parliament had lost its power, seats in Parliament retained symbolic importance. If he could fill the seats with Fascists, Mussolini would prove his regime had popular support.

The election would give Catholics their first chance to vote without guilt, and the Church urged all Catholics to go to the polls. A strong vote would mean strong approval for the recently signed Vatican treaty.

The ballot was simple. Italians could vote either for or against the Fascist regime. The election turned into the biggest in Italian history. Of those eligible, 89.63 percent went to the polls. The government received 8,517,838 "yes" votes against just 135,773 "no" votes.

An elated Mussolini could now turn his attention to some of Italy's serious problems. He used a method that combined old-fashioned power politics with modern advertising techniques. It usually worked.

He told the world he was going to make the trains run on time, and without making a great deal of change in the system, the rail service did indeed begin to be more reliable.

When Italy's economy slumped in the depression of 1929,

Mussolini countered with "The Battle of the Lira." The Fascist press called for wage reductions and other sacrifices to hold up the value of the national currency. "Heroes" of the battle who made the recommended sacrifices were singled out for interviews. Often their pictures would be taken as they shook hands with Il Duce.

Next came "The Battle of Grain," designed to reduce Italy's dependence on imported food. The press urged farmers to increase production. The government gave awards to those provinces harvesting the most of certain crops. Bronze, silver, and gold stars were awarded to farmers who met or exceeded production quotas.

Pictures appeared in the papers almost daily showing Mussolini dancing with farm workers, Mussolini receiving a farmhand's pay, Mussolini on a threshing machine, or Mussolini driving a horse cart loaded with produce. The campaign was a great success. In one year, grain imports alone were reduced by 102 million tons from the previous year.

Land reclamation in several different provinces gave Mussolini's campaigns local flavor and boosted the competitive spirit. Swamps were drained, irrigation systems were built, and brushland was cleared. The government claimed at one point that nine million new acres of land were brought into production. Of course, the new land also reduced dependence on food imports.

Reclamation of the Pontine Marshes near Rome, a huge undertaking, received international publicity. The marshes, one hundred and fifty thousand acres of swamp and mud, had been a source of malaria and other diseases since Roman times. Mussolini launched the Pontine reclamation campaign in November 1931. He rounded up the best engineers in the country to design a drainage system, and within a few months, as the network of drains spread, plowed fields and new towns began to appear. Mussolini seemed to be working a miracle, a well-publicized miracle.

Eventually, some seventy-five thousand new inhabitants, drawn from poor regions of Italy, were settled on the productive Pontine Plain. Even some of Mussolini's severest critics hailed the achievement. Indeed, the fertile farmlands remain today as a valuable legacy of Mussolini's energy and determination.

For Italian citizens, the much-publicized campaigns filled a psychological need. Under the Fascist regime, political debate could be dangerous. The government campaigns gave the people something safer to talk about.

Every region of the country had at least one government project. Road or bridge construction, drainage or irrigation systems, or new buildings provided employment as well as conversation. Mussolini, who officiated at many ground-breaking ceremonies, won gratitude everywhere—almost everywhere.

Reclamation in Rome, though, was a disaster. By clearing large sections of the Old City for public housing, he destroyed buildings that were both beautiful and historically valuable. The new buildings that went up in these areas were generally ugly. In architecture, Mussolini had the notion that big was everything.

His birth-rate campaign also was a flop. Mussolini seemed to be the only Italian favoring a population increase. Italy had problems enough feeding and sheltering the people it had, but Mussolini, apparently thinking more people meant more power, wanted to raise the population from forty million to fifty million by the middle of the century.

He tried to encourage marriage by placing a special tax on bachelors. To encourage births, he gave prizes to the mothers with the most children in each town and city of Italy. It was another all-out campaign. Government health programs for mothers and infants did improve, but the national birth rate declined.

Mussolini's rearmament campaign, while moderately successful, won little applause. He believed that Italy would become great only through force of arms. The government, however, could barely maintain its peacetime army and navy. Just the same, Mussolini warned the Italian people that they must prepare for war, and the gradual build-up of arms began.

MEANWHILE, MUCH WAS happening in neighboring countries. Hitler and his National Socialist (Nazi) party were gaining fanatical followers in Germany. Several Nazi leaders visited Italy to observe the Fascist regime and win friends in Rome. Mussolini, whose distrust of France had turned to hatred, looked upon Germany as a possible ally. At the same time, he was careful to stay on friendly terms with England. Someday he would have to take sides, but that day must not come until Italy was a military power.

FOREIGN AFFAIRS began to get more of Mussolini's attention when a young diplomat joined his family. Edda, the Mussolinis' beautiful but willful daughter, had a talent for bringing home unsuitable boyfriends. The latest had displayed his crude manners by asking Mussolini what Edda's dowry would be. Il Duce gave the suitor such a chilly glare that the boy departed in haste.

Mussolini discussed the problem with brother Arnaldo, his closest friend and adviser. Arnaldo had a practical suggestion. Why not marry Edda to the son of their old friend Count Costanzo Ciano? Mussolini had known the count since the early days of fascism. The count had given the party some much needed respectability, and he had always been willing to help. It was Count Ciano who had tried to negotiate a last-minute compromise with the king on the eve of the march to Rome.

Despite their long association, Mussolini was surprised to hear that the count had a son. His name was Galeazzo. He had worked as a journalist and later tried to write plays. Then he had joined the Italian foreign service. He had a talent for diplomacy and soon became one of the service's most promising young men. He was intelligent, popular, good looking, and a loyal Fascist.

At the time Arnaldo mentioned him, Galeazzo Ciano was vice consul in the Italian embassy in China. Mussolini directed that he be brought home and transferred to the Italian embassy office in the Vatican where everyone, including Edda, could have a look at him.

Edda liked him on first sight and agreed to marry him.

No time was lost. Rachele, who had never given a dinner party in her life, suddenly faced the prospect of entertaining the nobility. Luckily, Mussolini had recently moved his family from a crowded apartment into Villa Torlonia, a mansion surrounded by lawns and gardens.

But the surroundings were still new to Rachele, and she had only one servant to help her prepare the meal. All went well, however, and the happy parents set a date for the marriage— April 24, 1930.

Five hundred dignitaries attended a garden reception at the villa the day before the wedding. Bishops and cardinals, ambassadors from many nations, government officials, and party leaders, all in splendid dress, wandered through the garden chatting and sipping drinks. Although Mussolini's rough, revolutionary days seemed far behind, he was not comfortable in society. In a quiet moment, he told his two older sons, Vittorio and Bruno, that neither of them could expect such fanfare when they married.

Next day, Edda and Galeazzo were married in Rome's Church of San Giuseppe. The wedding gifts were a treasure of silverware, precious jewels, and furniture. Mussolini gave his daughter a rather humble gold and malachite rosary.

It was a strange marriage. Ciano had mistresses. Edda spent a great deal of time at card parties. Their different lifestyles kept them apart, sometimes in separate homes, but they were, in their own way, devoted to each other.

To no one's surprise, young Ciano advanced rapidly in the foreign service. Actually, he would have advanced on his own, but the marriage certainly speeded promotions. Mussolini often asked the energetic and well-informed Ciano for advice on foreign matters.

At the time of Edda's marriage, Mussolini's family was complete: Vittorio was fifteen and Bruno, seven. Another son, Romano, had been born in 1927, and Anna Maria, the infant, was only a year old. Mussolini, meanwhile, continued to have mistresses. Rachele was aware of his infidelities, but tried to ignore them.

THE YEAR 1931 brought renewed conflict with the Church. The issue was Catholic Action, a Church-sponsored youth group with chapters in nearly every town and city of Italy. Sports were a major part of the program, but Catholic Action also taught Christian morality. Its major fault was being far more popular than the Fascist youth organizations.

Something had to be done. In March of 1931 the Fascist press began calling Catholic Action an antigovernment organization. A few days later, Mussolini banned Catholic Action meetings, and in April Catholic Action was attacked in a major speech by the secretary of the Fascist party. By May, the Fascist press demanded closure of Catholic Action chapters. In the same month, police began boarding up doors of chapter houses and anti-Catholic demonstrations were staged by the government.

The pope fought back. He suspended celebration of feast days and wrote a strong anti-Fascist letter that was published in the Vatican newspaper. The newspaper went on sale five hours earlier than usual to avoid government confiscation.

Mussolini countered by ordering all Fascists participating in Catholic Action to resign from it or else give up their party membership. Because party membership was necessary for getting and holding a government job, thousands were forced to resign from Catholic Action.

It seemed that all of Mussolini's work for improved Church relations was in jeopardy when silence suddenly fell on the dispute. Was Mussolini having second thoughts about fighting the Church? Yes, indeed! The pope had secretly threatened to excommunicate Il Duce.

The threat was not revealed until years later. All the public knew was that Mussolini was suddenly willing to compromise. And he won a favorable settlement. Catholic Action was allowed to continue, but the Church agreed to restrict its activities to religious teaching only. It had to give up its popular sports sponsorships, leaving that field entirely to Fascist youth groups.

Despite the favorable outcome, renewal of hostilities with the Church had depressed him, and before 1931 ended Mussolini suffered a deep personal loss. His brother Arnaldo, who had been in failing health for several months, had a heart attack and died on December 21.

Since childhood, Arnaldo had been Mussolini's closest companion and confidant. He had respected Arnaldo's opinion and relied on his advice. His death left Il Duce very much alone in a world that was fast becoming less friendly.

13

Expansion

ADOLF HITLER came to power in Germany on January 30, 1933. Mussolini, who had ruled Italy for eleven years, had mixed feelings about his northern counterpart. Of course, he was pleased that another man had followed his path to power. Hitler's national socialism closely paralleled Italy's fascism. But Hitler's ambitions for expansion were well known. Would Nazi Germany one day try to add Italy to its empire?

Hitler's request for an early meeting with Il Duce to discuss matters of international policy, therefore, sent waves of worry through the Palazzo Venezia.

"International policy," as Il Duce and his aides knew, meant the future of Austria. The continued independence of Austria was important to Italy. Small as it was, Austria provided both a political and a military buffer between Germany and Italy.

Austria, however, was threatened the moment Hitler came to power. The Nazi creed promoted expansion, or *anschluss*. In his speeches, Hitler had often roused the emotion of crowds by saying that Germany must have more land to meet its destiny as a great nation. As the first step toward destiny, he said, Austria, which already contained a large population of Germans, must be taken.

Mussolini did not want to share a border with Germany.

Furthermore, Il Duce was on good terms with the Austrian government. He regarded Engelbert Dollfuss, the Austrian chancellor, as a personal friend, and had already promised Italian support if and when Austrian independence should be threatened.

Mussolini met Hitler in Venice on June 14, 1934. It was the first of many meetings between the two dictators and was perhaps the least successful.

Hitler, who had been advised by aides not to wear a uniform, appeared in a floppy felt hat and a wrinkled raincoat. He felt painfully untidy when standing next to Mussolini, whose smartly tailored uniform of the Fascist militia made him glow with authority.

The three-day schedule included sightseeing tours, public speeches, and private conferences. Hitler was impressed with Mussolini's speeches, which were well received by Venice crowds, but the Fuehrer would not play the role of junior statesman. In their private conferences, he talked almost nonstop, setting the pattern for all future meetings with Mussolini.

Hitler advised Mussolini to stop trying to protect Austria. The Fuehrer stated flatly that he wanted Chancellor Dollfuss replaced. Mussolini's protests were drowned under Hitler's flow of German.

Mussolini, proud that he knew some German, had refused an interpreter and undoubtedly misunderstood much of Hitler's rapid and incessant talk. And Hitler may not have understood Mussolini's rare statements. At one point when Hitler paused for breath, Il Duce declared that it was folly to persecute the Jews. Hitler either failed to understand or chose to ignore the statement. Anti-Semitism was another part of the Nazi creed.

Because of misunderstanding, Hitler returned to Berlin thinking that German acquisition of Austria had Mussolini's approval. Mussolini returned to Rome confirmed in his distrust of Hitler.

The distrust deepened fifteen days after the meeting when Nazi thugs, acting on Hitler's orders, murdered several high-ranking German politicians. Among the victims of "The Night of the Long Knives," as it became known, were men who had helped Hitler to power. He had them killed because he feared that they might one day threaten his authority.

Mussolini, who had met some of the victims, was still stunned by this treachery when tragic news came from Austria. On the morning of July 25, 1934, Nazi gunmen entered Chancellor Dollfuss's office, shot him as he sat at his desk, and left him bleeding to death.

By coincidence, on the day he was shot, Dollfuss had planned to fly to Italy for another meeting with Mussolini. In fact, Frau Dollfuss and her children were already in Italy awaiting the arrival of the chancellor. It was Mussolini's chore to bring news of the tragedy to the family.

Angry and humiliated, he then took two bold steps. He ordered Italian troops to mobilize on the Austrian border, and he sent a wire to the Austrian government promising that Italy would defend Austrian independence. He expected France and England to send similar wires, but they failed to take any action. Fuming with contempt for the western democracies, Mussolini was left to face Germany alone.

The German army, however, was not yet prepared for war, and Mussolini's bold stand was enough to force Hitler to reverse his plans abruptly.

The Nazi press, which had prepared gleeful special editions to announce Dollfuss's death and the fall of Austria, was ordered at the last minute to cancel publication. After quick revisions, the papers headlined a statement from Hitler condemning Dollfuss's assassination.

The assassins themselves, who had been assured of safe refuge in Germany, were arrested on Hitler's orders and turned over to the Austrian government for trial. And as a final gesture of conciliation, Hitler recalled the German ambassador and sent a replacement with instructions to seek improved relations with Austria.

Mussolini, emerging as a hero in the world press, won praise from England and grudging admiration from France.

He gained so much goodwill that he decided it was safe to proceed with his own ambitious plans for empire, plans that would send almost a million Italians two thousand miles from home. Il Duce had decided to add Abyssinia to Italy's East African colonies.

A RUGGED LAND of four-hundred thousand square miles on the southwest shore of the Red Sea, Abyssinia had special meaning to Italians. It was there in 1896 that the Italian army suffered a bloody and humiliating defeat. The battle of Adowa left six thousand Italian dead and reduced Italy's East African holdings to thin slivers of coastal territory—Eritrea on the north and Italian Somaliland to the south of Abyssinia. Thanks to the Adowa defeat, this land of high mountains and vast plains, known today as Ethiopia, remained an independent monarchy.

Italians wanted revenge, but Mussolini had other reasons for war. He believed Italy could not become a world power without large colonies. The status of France and England, he thought, was due largely to their colonies. Public opinion seemed to support him. In his speeches, whenever he compared Italy's destiny with the empire of Roman times, he always received an ovation. A purely political reason for war was that it would divert attention from domestic problems. Although the economy was gradually improving, Italy still ranked highest among European nations in unemployment, poverty, illiteracy, and disease.

And there was a personal reason for war. Mussolini felt challenged by Hitler's rapid rise in Germany and by his expansionist policies. Il Duce wanted Italy's conquests to begin while Hitler was still sharpening his sword.

The main obstacle to Mussolini's plan was Haile Selassie, Abyssinia's new emperor. A tireless ambassador for his country, he had collected friends throughout the capitals of Europe. His work had not been easy, in part because slavery was still practiced in Abyssinia. Just the same, Haile Selassie had won membership for his country in the League of Nations, and he expected the League to defend his country against aggression.

Mussolini knew the League might oppose him, but he reasoned that its most influential members, France and England, both had African colonies. On what moral ground could they object to Italy's colonial ambitions?

Mussolini failed to realize, however, that the colonial era was all but over and that self-rule for Africa loomed on the political horizon. Independent Abyssinia symbolized and provided the guiding example of self-rule. In this light, Mussolini's claim that Abyssinia was a threat to its neighbors sounded like a joke.

Mussolini, however, began to turn Eritrea, Italy's small colony on Abyssinia's northern border, into an armed camp. He claimed that Haile Selassie was about to invade Eritrea. The truth was that Haile Selassie did not have enough men under arms to defend his borders. But a border clash between an Italian garrison and Abyssinian border guards gave Mussolini the excuse for aggression that he had been hoping for.

The incident occurred on December 5, 1934, at Wal-Wal, a watering spot near the border of Italian Somaliland. Although Wal-Wal was actually inside Abyssinian territory, the Italians had long maintained a fort there. The trouble started when the Italian officer commanding the fort spotted a native patrol and, fearing attack, sent for reinforcements. Before help could arrive, the natives, provoked by the fort commander's reaction, attacked. The defenders suffered heavy losses but managed to save the outpost.

As soon as news of the fight reached Mussolini he stepped up war preparations. More troops and equipment were sent to

Eritrea. Early in 1935 General Emilio de Bono, recently named high commissioner of East Africa, set up military headquarters in Massaua, the port city of Eritrea. He was to invade Abyssinia as soon as the rainy season ended. Meanwhile, he received and trained the Italian troops swarming into the port. By the end of May almost a million Italian soldiers were stationed in the small colony.

France and England were too timid to interfere. Although they opposed Mussolini's venture, the western democracies feared that a strong stand might force him into an alliance with Hitler. French ambassadors were so indecisive that Mussolini assumed he had French approval. English diplomats could not agree on an official position soon enough to change Mussolini's mind.

Finally the skies over East Africa cleared and the dry season began. On October 2, 1935, Mussolini strode onto the balcony of the Palazzo Venezia, placed his fists on his hips, and smiled down at the cheering crowd.

"A solemn hour is about to strike in the history of the Fatherland," he said. "Not only is the army marching towards its objective, but forty million Italians are marching in unison with the army, all united because there is an attempt to commit against them the blackest of all injustices, to rob them of a place in the sun. . . . With Ethiopia we have been patient for forty years. Now enough!"

A deafening cheer rose from the square. The next day the Italian army crossed the border into Abyssinia. There was little opposition.

It took just three days to engulf Adowa, and little more than a month after the attack began, the Italian front was well established some eighty miles inside Abyssinia. General de Bono planned to regroup at this point, but Mussolini would not allow it. He recalled de Bono and replaced him with Marshal

Pietro Badoglio with orders to complete the campaign quickly.

Mussolini had good reason for haste. The League of Nations, under pressure from England and France, had reacted faster and with more vigor than anticipated. It had declared Italy an aggressor nation and called upon all member nations to stop shipping major trade commodities to Italy. Luckily for Italy, oil was not at the moment included on the list of banned cargoes. And luckily, the Suez Canal was not closed to Italian ships. But threat of these crippling restrictions worried Il Duce.

Early in 1936 Marshal Badoglio opened a hard-hitting campaign that crushed organized resistance in four months. On May 5, Italian troops marched into Addis Ababa, the capital of Abyssinia. Haile Selassie fled for his life. On May 9 a proud Mussolini announced from the balcony of the Palazzo Venezia that Adowa had been avenged. Most of his victory speech, however, was drowned out by thundering cheers.

"Duce! Duce! Duce!"

At last it seemed that he had won the heart of every Italian citizen.

Although guerrilla fighting would continue, Abyssinia was now regarded by most Italians as part of the colonial empire, and it was all but forgotten as world attention turned to the Spanish Civil War.

SPAIN'S REVOLT was led by Francisco Franco, a right-wing army general who had seen long service in Spanish Morocco. His invasion force, made up mostly of army regulars from North Africa, began a slow, bloody march on Madrid. His goal was to overthrow Spain's recently established republic.

Having been ruled for centuries by monarchs, Spain had adopted a democratic republic almost as an experiment. It had not been a great success. Spain's powerful land-owning aristocracy felt threatened by the new government's land reform plans. The Catholic Church, which had long dominated religious thought and practices, feared the republic's liberal religious policies. Franco thus had the support of the aristocracy and the Church, two powerful factions. He also got support from Italy.

Mussolini began giving Franco help just a few days after the fighting began. Actually, he had promised it almost eighteen months before the first shots were fired. And because Franco called himself a Fascist, Mussolini kept the promise.

The war started on July 18, 1936. Within just a few days, Mussolini sent twelve airplanes to help escort troopships from Africa to Spain. He consulted no one else in his government, not even the king. Mussolini thought the war would be so short that he could easily keep Italian aid a secret.

On July 29, however, two of the Italian planes he had sent to Spain developed engine trouble and had to land in French Morocco. Soon the world press, overwhelmingly sympathetic to the republic, headlined the news of Italian aid.

Mussolini made no further attempt to hide Italy's role. Instead, he increased it. His worry was that Franco would win so quickly that Italy would receive little credit or gratitude when Franco came to power.

Volunteers, drawn from the ranks of the regular Italian army, were quickly rushed to Spain. Ill-armed and poorly trained, they proved more of a handicap to Franco than a help. But Mussolini kept sending men.

Hitler, meanwhile, did nothing. The crafty Fuehrer knew that the western democracies and Russia would side with the republic and thus become indirect enemies of Italy. The longer fighting continued in Spain, Hitler reasoned, the closer Italy would come to a German alliance. Hitler eventually did send aid to Franco, some aircraft and the much-publicized Condor Legion, but the Fuehrer's main goal was to prolong the civil war.

The war dragged on. As Hitler suspected, the Republicans won support from the western democracies and Russia. The volunteer Lincoln Brigade came from America to fight against fascism. It was a merciless war. Both sides committed atrocities that shocked the world. In a new pattern of air attack, civilians became primary victims of bombing raids. The bloody pattern would be amplified and repeated again and again in World War II.

Italy, its supply of raw materials low after Abyssinia, had to scrimp to help Franco. Just the same, by the end of 1937 Mussolini had sent every aircraft he could spare and thirty-seven thousand men to Spain. The Italian economy suffered. Mussolini's popularity, so high after the African success, sank sharply, but he could see no way out of his commitment.

MEANWHILE, HE WAS distracted from affairs of state by a new love affair. Clara Petacci, a beautiful, vivacious woman who had recently separated from her husband, was young enough to be Mussolini's daughter. But both of them were moonstruck. Mussolini talked to Petacci every morning on the telephone, and at 3 o'clock every afternoon she arrived at the Palazzo Venezia to wait for Il Duce to finish his work. Gossip about the affair further damaged Il Duce's reputation, but this was no passing affair. They were to remain lovers the rest of their lives.

Love may have made him reckless, for at the height of the Spanish war he ordered Italian submarines to attack English ships carrying supplies to Republican Spain. He canceled the order as soon as England threatened retaliation, but relations between Italy and the western democracies seemed to have deteriorated beyond repair.

Hitler decided the time had come for another grab at Austria.

14

Hitler

ADOLF HITLER'S influence over Benito Mussolini was Italy's big tragedy. Although neither man realized it at first, there was more in their characters to keep them apart than bring them together.

Mussolini often changed his mind. He was troubled by self-doubts. Hitler knew his own mind perfectly, and if he ever had a doubt, he suffered it in silence. Although Mussolini posed in the public as the strongman, a symbol of power with dramatic gestures and loud, positive statements, he gave up that role completely in private. He could be warm and human, with charming manners and a ready laugh. He was childishly curious about people. He liked to welcome visitors and usually enjoyed listening to their opinions.

Hitler, on the other hand, never changed roles. In public or in private, he was the same. Talking incessantly, he rarely listened to anyone. Hitler's ambitious zeal was contagious. He was surrounded by followers who shared his ambitions. Mussolini himself caught the zeal.

In the beginning, both men recognized and gloried in their common roots. Hitler organized his Nazi Brownshirts along the military lines pioneered by Mussolini and his Blackshirts. Both men played on the fear of communism to gain followers. The Nazis used other Fascist tactics, including violence and the threat of violence, to quiet opposition. And Hitler, like Mussolini, had read Machiavelli.

Hitler at first saw Mussolini as a strong and resourceful leader and worked hard to gain his friendship and alliance. Of course, Hitler needed Italy on his side for the Austrian venture to succeed.

Although Hitler puzzled Mussolini, Il Duce willingly accepted an invitation to visit the Fuehrer in Germany. Hitler planned the meeting with all his attention. It would be the most splendid state visit the modern world had ever seen. There would be parades with marching bands, troops of infantry, and rumbling war machines. There would be war exercises. There would be speeches, banquets, and entertainment. And there would be streets lined with more bunting than had ever before fluttered in Berlin—fifty-five thousand square yards of it.

Sent to Berlin to help with preparations, son-in-law Ciano heard Hitler praise Mussolini, the Italian people, their great past, and their promising future. Using all the charm he had, the Fuehrer listed the advantages of an Italian-German alliance, concluding that it would be a bulwark against eastern communism and western democracy.

Ciano was so impressed that he signed a secret pact promising Italian cooperation on many diplomatic issues. Although Mussolini never revealed the terms of this pact, he apparently endorsed it because soon after Ciano returned to Rome, Il Duce spoke of a Berlin-Rome "axis." During the coming years of turmoil, "Axis" would become a common word in the newspaper headlines of the world.

With almost one hundred journalists and Fascist officials, Mussolini boarded the train for Germany on September 23, 1937. He was greeted on the station platform in Munich with a warm handshake from Hitler. For the next five days, the Fuehrer rarely left Mussolini's side.

After lunching with Nazi leaders, the dictators watched the first of many long parades. For hour after hour units of the Nazi

Labor Service, the Nazi party, and the Nazi Youth marched with well-practiced precision past the review stand. Mussolini felt highly honored and deeply impressed.

Next, the two men with their many attendants and journalists boarded a special train that sped them to an army base where a military exercise was in progress. They watched a sham battle that included a simulated poison gas attack.

The following day, the party traveled to Essen and inspected the huge Krupp munitions factory. Tanks, guns, and a seemingly endless supply of ammunition poured from the assembly lines. Mussolini could hardly believe that one factory could produce such a volume and variety of arms.

By the time the party headed for Berlin, Mussolini had begun to look upon Hitler as a wizard of military organization and political power. They traveled in two trains, one for each dictator. The trains ran side by side until just before reaching the new Berlin depot that had been built for the occasion. Then Hitler's train shot ahead, making it possible for him to greet Mussolini on the platform as Il Duce stepped from his train.

The two then rode to the center of Berlin on streets lined with thousands of German and Italian flags. One broad avenue was bordered by four rows of white pillars topped with golden eagles and Nazi swastikas and Fascist *fasces*. The green, red, and white of Italy hung in bunting from every building along the route.

The city teemed with people. Shops and offices throughout Berlin had been closed early for the occasion, and special trains had brought thousands of people to the city from outlying districts. Il Duce's official bodyguard, made up of sixty thousand Nazi storm troopers, lined the route. City police, reinforced by crack units from Saxony, also stood guard. The crowd, playing its role on cue, cheered lustily as Hitler and Mussolini, standing side by side in an open car, led the procession slowly toward the heart of the city.

Throughout most of the next day, eight hundred thousand men and women, each carrying a day's supply of food, filed onto a huge athletic field on the outskirts of Berlin. Some had been marching since 4 A.M. to attend the afternoon program. At 4 P.M. Hitler and Mussolini mounted the speaker's stand before the cheering Berliners. Mussolini delivered a carefully prepared speech in which he declared that Germany and Italy were united for peace and, if necessary, for war. Henceforth, he declared, one hundred and fifty million people would be forever united in a common purpose.

Few in the huge crowd understood Il Duce's German, and throughout the speech, a violent thunderstorm raged. But the people were there to cheer Italy's visiting dictator and cheer they did.

Next day, after watching another long parade of goose-stepping German troops, Mussolini and his party boarded a train for home. He returned to Rome a changed man, changed at least in his view of Germany and its dynamic new leader.

Here was a nation that had recovered from defeat to become once again the leading military power in Europe, and here was a leader who was eager to use that power. Mussolini was convinced that Italy would benefit from German friendship.

Wishing to match German military might in any way he could, Mussolini ordered the Italian army to adopt the goose step whenever it marched on parade. King Victor Emmanuel III protested the order strongly but in vain. Meanwhile, Mussolini began planning for Hitler's visit to Rome, a visit the two leaders had already agreed should take place in early May of 1938.

While in Germany, Mussolini had heard no mention of Austria. But it was clear to him that any interference in Hitler's plans would cost Hitler's friendship. Mussolini's state visit had thus accomplished exactly what Hitler intended it should.

The average German was skeptical about an Italian alliance. Some Germans liked to joke that because the western democracies were allied with Italy during World War I, it was only fair that Germany take on the responsibility in the next war.

Hitler did not take this attitude at all. He moved quickly to strengthen Italian relations. Less than three weeks after the state visit, Joachim von Ribbentrop, Hitler's roving ambassador, arrived in Rome to get Il Duce's signature on an anti-Russian pact already signed by Japan and Germany. Mussolini did not hesitate in adding his name.

On December 11, following Germany's lead, Mussolini took Italy out of the League of Nations. Meanwhile, without confiding in Mussolini, Hitler expanded his ambitions by planning the invasion of Czechoslovakia as well as Austria.

Early in 1938, Hitler called Kurt von Schuschnigg, the Austrian chancellor, to Berlin and bullied him into signing a pact that virtually surrendered Austrian independence. In Vienna, news of the pact undermined most of the chancellor's remaining support. His last hope was a special election, or plebiscite, that would give Austrian citizens a chance to show their desire for independence. When the chancellor asked Mussolini to support a plebiscite, however, Il Duce lamely advised Schuschnigg to be patient. The Nazi pressure, Mussolini shamelessly predicted, was sure to decline.

Schuschnigg, disheartened by Mussolini's indifference, went ahead just the same and set March 13 for the vote on Austria's future. Hitler could not allow the free election to be held, and so, in the early hours of March 12, Nazi tanks began rolling toward the Austrian border. In a long wire to Mussolini, Hitler told of the need to "restore order" in Austria by invading the country. He asked for Il Duce's approval. Although Mussolini resented the loss of Austria, he endorsed invasion.

Hitler was jubilant. "Tell Mussolini I will never forget him for this," Hitler told an aide. "Never, never, never, whatever happens. . . . "

A protest from Mussolini or a show of strength by England

or France might have saved Austria. The German army was not yet ready for all-out war. Hitler was acting largely on bluff, and he won.

ITALIANS WERE generally shocked by the easy Nazi success in Austria. Why had Il Duce abandoned an old friend? What now would keep Germany from marching into Italy? Mussolini's prestige sank to the lowest level it had been since Matteotti's murder.

He told the Chamber of Deputies that Italy had never assumed any obligation, formal or informal, to defend Austrian independence. He added that any independence needing the help of Italy or any other foreign country to save it did not deserve the name. Finally, he assured the deputies that Italy had nothing to fear from Germany.

Despite his public assurances, however, Mussolini's distrust of Hitler revived and he began to seek improved relations with England. But the civil war still raged in Spain, and England by now had decided to close diplomatic discussions with Italy until Mussolini withdrew aid from Franco. It was an impasse.

Meanwhile, as May 1938 approached, security for Hitler's visit to Rome took more and more of Il Duce's attention. Germany sent an advance force of eighty detectives and some five hundred undercover agents to pose as tourists from other countries. These agents, all with a good understanding of Italian, were to report any anti-German talk they might hear. Well before Hitler arrived in Rome some six thousand anti-German citizens were jailed.

Security measures, however, could not assure a successful meeting. It started badly when Hitler stepped from the train and was greeted, not by Mussolini, but by a cool handshake from the king, a man openly opposed to Hitler and his Nazis.

No one had explained to the Fuehrer that the king remained Italy's chief representative in state affairs. Hitler was dumbstruck to see Mussolini standing at the edge of the crowd observing the ceremony. Il Duce did not even join the procession to the palace. It was a deadly quiet procession. Only a few curious people stood along the route. Hitler was disgusted.

Although he was official host for the six-day visit, the king did nothing to hide his dislike of Hitler. The Church gave no welcome at all. The official Vatican newspaper printed no word of the visit. The pope closed the famous Vatican Museum and retired to his country estate for six days.

Despite these chilly winds, the climate of the visit soon warmed. Hitler was enchanted by peasant dancers in colorful costumes, dancing to native music. The military parades and a review of the Italian fleet were impressive. At lavish banquets, Mussolini, not the king, played the congenial host.

In an after-banquet speech at the Palazzo Venezia, Hitler praised Mussolini's "Roman State" and compared it to the Roman Empire of ancient times. The Fuehrer received the most applause, however, when he promised that Germany would never violate the Italian border.

Hitler and Mussolini went together from Rome to Florence, where the crowds were more enthusiastic and there was no unfriendly royal host.

When the two dictators parted at the Florence railroad station Mussolini said, "Henceforth, no force will be able to separate us."

Hitler made no response, but observers said that his eyes filled with tears.

Like Mussolini's visit to Germany, Hitler's visit to Italy was so full of ceremony and public appearances that there was little time for discussion. Even though Germany was about to invade Czechoslovakia, Hitler made only brief mention of that country. For his part, Mussolini said just enough to let Hitler know that Italy would not interfere.

Hitler had a strange effect on Mussolini. When with the Fuehrer, Il Duce was likely to agree to anything that might be proposed. When on his own, however, Mussolini voiced many doubts and worries.

But there were apparently no second thoughts on Hitler's recommendation that Jews be eliminated in Italy just as they were being eliminated in Germany. This was surprising on two counts. In all of Italy there were just thirty-seven thousand Jews, hardly enough to draw attention, and Mussolini was not a bigot.

In his early days in politics he had condemned anti-Semitism. Angelica Balabanoff and Margherita Sarfatti, the two women who had influenced his politics most strongly, were both Jewish, and he never spoke of any personal experience that might have made him prejudiced.

Just the same, two months after Hitler's visit, Mussolini issued a manifesto describing a "pure Italian race" that must not be corrupted by Jews or any other non-Italians. A few weeks later, the manifesto was backed up with new laws. One law, aimed specifically at Jews trying to flee from Nazi persecution, made it illegal for foreign Jews to live in Italy or Libya. Other laws made it illegal for Jews to teach school, to join the armed forces, to own more than 123 acres of land, or to have a business with more than one hundred employees. A Jew could not marry an Italian nor join the Fascist party—a party that had once welcomed Jews.

The laws often were not enforced to the letter, but they were on the books.

At the time, however, Italy's Jews were not Mussolini's major concern. He was desperately worried that Hitler would start a major war before Italy was ready. Although a war in alliance with the powerful Germans promised Italy many fruits of conquest, Hitler was moving far too fast. Italy's military strength had been drained by the long involvement in Spain. It would take years to rebuild the army, but Hitler talked as if war were just months away. He now seem ready to risk total war for Czechoslovakia.

Clara Petacci [National Archives]

Mothers presented their children for Mussolini's approval during a 1937 patriotic demonstration in Rome. Despite his many affairs, Mussolini was a family man with a real affection for children. [UPI/Bettmann News Photos]

Hitler and Mussolini met for many strategic conferences. Hitler usually held the pointer and did most of the talking. Here, Marshal Hermann Goering is on Hitler's left. [National Archives]

Otto Skorzeny
[National Archives]

Walter Audisio, the man who shot Mussolini and Petacci,
went into politics after the war. Here he speaks at a
Communist rally. Later he was elected to the Italian
parliament. [National Archives]

When Nazi paratroopers rescued Mussolini from his
mountaintop prison, he thought his political career was over,
but Hitler had other ideas. [from *Pictorial History of the
Second World War*, NY: Wise & Co., Inc., 1946]

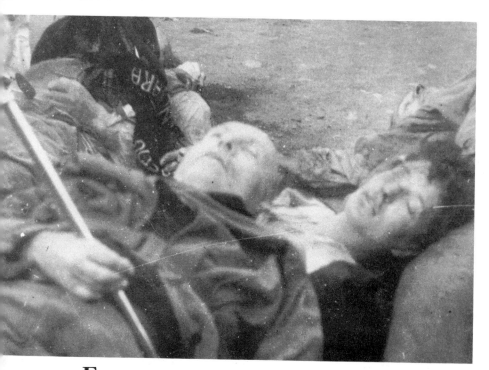

Fascism in Italy came to a violent end with the death of
Mussolini. His body rests here on top of Clara Petacci's.
[National Archives]

In the final indignity, the bodies of Mussolini, Petacci, and
others are hung from girders in a Milan square to be reviled
by angry Italians. [UPI/Bettmann News Photos, Courtesy
of the National Archives]

15

Hall of Mirrors

ALL THROUGH 1938, the last peaceful year of his rule, Mussolini was like a man trapped in a hall of mirrors. He could not advance because he did not know which way to go, and when he tried to escape, he only became more confused among the false images.

The Spanish Civil War dragged on without end. Although he fumed over Franco's slow progress, Mussolini continued to send men, arms, and supplies. His commitment had soured public opinion. At home and abroad, he was seen as a warmonger, no different from Hitler. Italians wanted peace. Wives and parents prayed for the men to be brought home from Spain.

It was not a good time for any more military pacts with foreign countries, particularly Nazi Germany, but Mussolini favored such a pact. Public opinion and the poor state of Italian arms, however, forced caution. Hitler's ambitions were bound to set off a general war, and Italy, because of Abyssinia and Spain, was not ready for a world war.

Mussolini thus faced a dilemma. On the one hand he feared that Hitler's war would begin before Italy could rebuild its armed strength. On the other hand, if he held back, Mussolini might miss the fruits of that war, such as the glory of conquest and new territory to add to his empire.

German foreign minister Ribbentrop and other Nazi officials had promised Il Duce that Germany would not start a major war until 1941 at the earliest. But Hitler himself had promised nothing. The Fuehrer was unpredictable. He had deliberately left Mussolini in the dark about Austria. Italy learned of the invasion only after it had begun.

Now, as 1938 ripened, it was obvious that Hitler intended to take Czechoslovakia into his realm. Invasion of Czechoslovakia might touch off the big war. It could happen soon, within weeks.

SMALL BUT IMPORTANT, Czechoslovakia stretched east and west across Central Europe like a bone, a fat bone that already seemed to be in the German mouth. The 49,357-square-mile nation had been carved out of the Austro-Hungarian Empire by World War I peace treaties that were designed to change the balance of power forever. Hitler claimed, just as he had done with Austria, that Germans living in Czechoslovakia were being treated as second-class citizens. Indeed, the country's mixed population was a problem. Slovaks and Czechs, the two majorities, had little in common except for their dislike of the Hungarian and German minorities.

Most Germans lived in the border region of Sudetenland. Nazi agents had long been at work there organizing campaigns for independence. Mass meetings and riots became common. To keep peace, the Czech government was forced to mobilize its army, and as soon as Czech soldiers moved into Sudetenland, Hitler claimed the Czechs were getting ready to invade Germany. It was a ridiculous claim, but it was excuse enough for Hitler to mobilize German troops on the Czech border to "defend" Germany.

Of course, the "defenders" were in reality the invaders. England and France, under treaty to defend Czechoslovakia, prepared for war. As the summer of 1938 drew to a close, all-out war seemed ready to erupt at any moment.

Mussolini, still trapped in the hall of mirrors, did not know what to do. He had already told Hitler that Italy would not interfere in Czechoslovakia, but he had not expected Hitler to move so quickly.

Now Hitler asked for help. He suggested that Mussolini mobilize troops on the French-Italian border. They would force France to hold back troops for defense that otherwise might be used to invade Germany when the war started. Il Duce wanted to help, but how could he tell Hitler that he did not have any troops to send north? Mussolini looked desperately for a way out of his dilemma.

The way came like a miracle. Neville Chamberlain, the English prime minister, called an international conference on the crisis and asked Mussolini to serve as peacemaker.

Mussolini accepted the invitation at once.

The conference was held in Munich, Germany, on September 29 and 30. The western democracies, wanting peace at any price, adopted a policy of such cowardly appeasement that "Munich" became a word of shame. Czechoslovakia, not even represented at the conference, was all but given to Hitler. Chamberlain, the idealistic dreamer, was no match for Hitler, the scheming devil. Mussolini, however, emerged as the man of peace.

The only delegate who did not need an interpreter, he scurried back and forth from Hitler to Chamberlain and from Chamberlain to Edouard Daladier, the chief French delegate. He explained demands and counter demands. He made recommendations. Hitler, who had been ready to fight, was impatient with talk, but at Mussolini's urging he agreed to withdraw his invasion force from the Czech border. In exchange, he was given Sudetenland. All delegates agreed that a plebiscite, or vote on independence, would be held in the rest of Czechoslovakia. Clearly, the people would vote to keep their independence, but Hitler did not intend to allow any elections.

Having no voice at the conference and all but abandoned by England and France, Czechoslovakia could no longer resist

Nazi pressure. A few weeks after Munich, Czech leaders surrendered the entire country to Germany.

Meanwhile, Mussolini went home a hero. On the route to Rome, cheering crowds lined the railroad tracks. The train stations were jammed with joyful people who hailed Il Duce as their peacemaker. Some fell to their knees the moment his train appeared. The king went north to meet and congratulate Mussolini at Florence. Mussolini was both pleased and puzzled, pleased over his revived popularity, but puzzled by his new role. He was not really a peacemaker. The demonstrations for peace actually disgusted him. Italy could never meet its destiny as a world power by making peace.

MUSSOLINI'S POPULARITY plummeted when the Nazis took all of Czechoslovakia, and everyone realized that Munich had been nothing more than a sham.

Munich had given Hitler a new opinion of Mussolini. The man could be an irksome meddler. Aware that he was out of favor with the Nazis, Mussolini needed some way to restore his prestige. It was not long in coming.

On March 28, 1939, Franco's forces occupied Madrid and put an end at last to the Spanish Civil War. It had taken three years, but Mussolini was finally free of his commitment to Franco. Italy could once again seek her destiny.

Mussolini and Ciano decided to begin by annexing Albania. It should be easy. Actually, Italy already controlled the small country across the Adriatic Sea. Although it had its own king and Parliament, Albania had not been considered an independent nation for several years. No other nations were pledged to defend it. An Italian conquest would be only symbolic, giving formal recognition to a situation that already existed.

Mussolini, however, spoke as if he were planning the most dramatic venture of his life. He first advised the German embassy that Italy demanded a free hand because Albania was a "family matter." This echoed the phrase used by Hitler when warning Mussolini not to interfere in the invasions of Austria and Czechoslovakia. Now the phrase sounded like a joke.

Ciano told the Germans, "The Duce declares that he is ready to go into Albania at once, even at the cost of setting fire to the European powder barrel. He is already making the necessary military preparations."

Clearly, Mussolini believed that the invasion of Albania would restore his prestige with Hitler. But the invasion, begun on April 7, 1939, which happened to be Good Friday, turned into a circus of mismanagement. The Italian troops were so poorly equipped, trained, and led that their very survival was a miracle.

General Guzzoni, who headed the invasion, had hoped to march at once from the coast four miles inland to seize Tirana, the Albanian capital. The march, however, was delayed for hours by confusion and poor communications. The Albanian government added further delay by suggesting a negotiated truce. The peace offer had to be relayed to Mussolini over civilian phone lines. There was no other link between Rome and the Italian army. With help from some puzzled telephone operators, Mussolini managed to tell Guzzoni to ignore the peace bid.

Meanwhile, chaos ruled in Tirana. It had been abandoned by the Albanian government. The prisons had been opened. Armed rioters and looters roamed the streets. Crowds outside the Italian embassy threatened to break it down and kill all Italians. Where was Guzzoni's army?

It did not reach the capital until the following morning, about twenty hours behind schedule. By then, responsible citizens of the city had already restored order. The Italians took possession of Tirana and ended the one-day Albanian war. Fortunately, no shots had been fired.

Ciano and Mussolini, knowing little about the traditions and economy of Albania, had no definite idea how it should be governed. Ciano said maybe Albanians should simply swear allegiance to Victor Emmanuel as their king and retain their existing Parliament and civil government. This made sense, but Mussolini and other Fascist leaders wanted the country ruled by Italians. As a consequence, Albania became a province ruled by people with little knowledge or interest in the country.

CONQUEST OF ALBANIA barely caused a stir among other nations. The western democracies, still trying to woo Mussolini away from Hitler, made very weak protests. Hitler congratulated Il Duce, but said the time for independent actions was over. Italy and Germany must make a military alliance.

Mussolini had already decided to sign the pact with Hitler, but now Ciano, once pro-German, advised caution. In just a few months, Ciano predicted, Hitler would invade Poland and ignite a world war. Italy, Ciano said, was not ready for war.

Nevertheless, in May 1939, Mussolini sent Ciano to Milan to discuss final details of the pact with Ribbentrop. The German foreign minister, glowing with goodwill and charm, assured Ciano there would be four or five more years of peace. As for Poland, Ribbentrop said, Germany was content to wait. Among these shameless lies Ribbentrop dropped a startling truth: Germany wanted a nonaggression treaty with Russia.

Mussolini took the news as further incentive to sign a pact with Germany. He had the foolish dream that Russia, as a partner in the Axis, might take on much of the military load of Hitler's ambitions and thus relieve Italy of a good deal of responsibility. Had he known Joseph Stalin, Communist Russia's cold-blooded leader, Mussolini would have run in terror from the prospect of a Russian alliance.

There was much pomp, ceremony, and press coverage in Berlin when Hitler and Ciano, as Il Duce's representative, finally signed the pact. It happened on May 22, 1939. Mussolini, calling it "the Pact of Steel," immediately ordered construction of six new battleships and several new munitions factories. Ciano pressed for more time, and top-ranking Nazis promised three years of peace even though they knew that the invasion of Poland was just four months away.

English ambassadors warned Mussolini of the swift approach of war. Even Italian ambassadors predicted the early invasion of Poland. Mussolini ignored all warnings and spent much effort trying to persuade Franco to join the Axis. Spain's dictator, however, was set on neutrality.

On June 17 Joseph Goebbels, Nazi minister of propaganda, accused Poland of suppressing the rights of German-speaking populations within its borders. Here was a repeat of the Nazis' usual preinvasion charges. Bernardo Attolico, Italy's ambassador in Berlin, demanded to know Germany's intentions in Poland. He even tried to arrange an emergency meeting on Poland between Mussolini and Hitler. Mussolini, however, refused to ask for a meeting and told Attolico not to succumb to war panic.

At the end of July, however, Mussolini finally seemed to wake from his dream. Had the Nazis been lying to him? He instructed Attolico to suggest a Polish peace conference. Perhaps Mussolini could once again play his heroic role as peacemaker.

Hitler, with mobilization of his Polish invasion force almost complete, turned down the suggestion for a conference.

From Berlin, Attolico's warnings finally began to alarm Mussolini. He ordered Ciano to go to Germany and do everything possible to delay the invasion. Ribbentrop met Ciano but refused to discuss war plans. Ciano reminded the German foreign minister about his promised three years of peace. Ribbentrop answered that the situation had changed. When Ciano asked what it was exactly that Germany wanted, Ribbentrop snapped, "We want war."

The next day Ciano heard the same thing from Hitler. The Fuehrer went on to observe cheerfully that it was good luck that both he and Il Duce were still young and vigorous enough to be effective in the coming conflict with England and France. When

Ciano tried to protest, Hitler suggested that this might be a good time for Italy to invade Yugoslavia.

Ciano stated flatly that Italy was not ready for war. Hitler shrugged and said that the invasion of Poland probably would not trigger war. Ciano, seeing he was being treated like a child, demanded that Hitler join Mussolini in a public statement assuring other nations of peace. Hitler said he would consider this the next day.

Ciano, however, was too angry to stay in Berlin another day. He returned to Rome and told Mussolini that Hitler had betrayed Italy. In his diary, Ciano wrote that he was "completely disgusted with the Germans, with their leader, with their way of doing things. They have betrayed and lied to us. Now they are dragging us into an adventure we do not want."

The Germans added to Ciano's fury by publishing the "news" that his visit had resulted in complete agreement between Italy and Germany on Poland's future.

Ciano told Mussolini to tear up the Pact of Steel, keep Italy out of the conflict, and become a leader for world peace. But Mussolini, still dreaming of the fruits of war, would not heed this sound advice. He still hoped Italy would become a military power. And if he tore up the Pact of Steel, what would keep Hitler from adding Italy to his list of acquisitions?

In a way, Ciano's protests sealed Poland's fate. Hitler realized that further delay of the invasion would only give Mussolini more time to think. The Fuehrer meanwhile sent Il Duce a long, friendly letter outlining German intentions in Poland and trying to explain why Italy had not been consulted prior to the Nazi pact with Russia. Hitler closed by asking for Mussolini's continued friendship and support.

Although the letter was intended to quiet Mussolini's fears, he saw it as a chance to ask for German aid. He wrote back to Hitler saying that Italy could give Germany support for a small Polish war, but lacked the raw materials and the arms to support a major war at this time.

Hitler was angry, but replied with the suggestion that Mussolini make a list of Italy's needs. Perhaps Germany could provide some raw materials.

Mussolini answered that he needed two million tons of steel, six million tons of coal, seven million tons of oil, and lesser amounts of copper, nickel, and thirteen other items. He also asked for 150 antiaircraft batteries. These items, Mussolini said, should be delivered before hostilities began.

Now it was Hitler's turn to feel betrayed. Italy's needs made it clear that Germany would have to face the western democracies alone. But the Fuehrer hid his anger and promised Mussolini that everything would be provided in due time.

Mussolini, having found an escape at last, answered that if the raw materials could not be provided at once, Italy would be forced to remain neutral.

Hitler, thoroughly impatient by now, managed again to keep his feelings in check. He wrote that he respected Mussolini's position, but asked him to keep it in silence.

"In my opinion, however," the Fuehrer wrote, "the prerequisite is that, at least until the outbreak of the struggle, the world should have no idea of the attitude Italy intends to adopt. I therefore cordially beg of you to support my struggle psychologically with your press and by other means. I would also ask you, Duce, if you possibly can, by demonstrative military measures, at least to compel Britain and France to tie down certain of their forces, or at all events to leave them in uncertainty."

Mussolini received this, the final letter in the exchange, on August 28, 1939. Three days later, without any advance notice to Rome, German troops invaded Poland, and World War II began.

16

War

WHEN GERMAN TROOPS invaded Poland on September 1, 1939, the deadly storm that was to last nearly six years spread quickly over Europe. For nine months, however, Italy was spared.

Mussolini, who loved his militant pose, was so ashamed of his neutrality that he would not speak of it. He called it "nonbelligerence." His role as peacemaker was also embarrassing, but he continued to seek some kind of accord even after Hitler asked him to stop.

On September 2, while German tanks were rumbling toward Warsaw, the Polish capital, Mussolini asked the major powers once more to consider a peace conference. The English ambassador replied that a conference was possible only if Germany withdrew its troops from Poland. Hitler, of course, would not agree, and the next day England and France declared war.

Although Mussolini watched restlessly from the sidelines, neutrality benefitted Italy's economy. The country was soon providing goods to both sides in the conflict. Italian shipping boomed. Neutrality became very popular with Italians, but Mussolini chose for once to ignore public opinion.

He feared that the war might end before Italy had a chance to become involved and reap some benefits. He itched to follow Hitler's suggestion and invade Yugoslavia.

On September 8 the Germans occupied Warsaw, and on the seventeenth Russian troops invaded from the east. Polish resistance crumbled. Mussolini tried once more to negotiate a truce. England said there was no turning back, and Mussolini, beginning to hear rumors of a German invasion of Belgium and Holland, gave up trying for peace.

Mussolini knew that if the invasion of Belgium and Holland took place, world opinion would condemn Germany. Italy's neutrality might be beneficial after all. For a time, he wished for and predicted a German defeat.

He allowed Ciano to make an anti-German speech before the Chamber of Deputies, and in a long letter to Hitler sent early in 1940, Mussolini condemned Germany's brutal treatment of Polish civilians, Germany's treaty with Russia, and Russia's November 30 invasion of Finland. He said Communist Russia was the true enemy of the Axis and that Hitler should seek the land he needed for his expansion policies by invading Russia.

Despite the critical tone of the letter, Mussolini concluded by promising his continued loyalty and friendship. Hitler delayed answering Il Duce's letter and sent instead a list of reasons for Italy's early entry into the war:

- Italy and Germany together could easily defeat France and England.
- Defeat of Germany, although unlikely, would be the death of fascism in Italy.
- If Italy failed to join the fight, it could not expect any spoils of victory.
- There was no danger of a second front because Russia had been neutralized by the nonaggression treaty.

Ciano warned Il Duce that Hitler's view of the military situation was far too simple, but Mussolini, despite many second thoughts, began gradually to strengthen his resolve to fight. No one else in Italy seemed at all interested in war. In fact, the peaceful nature of Italians frustrated Il Duce.

"We must keep them disciplined and in uniform from morning to night," he told an aide, "beat them and beat them and beat them. Have you ever seen a lamb become a wolf? The Italian race is a race of sheep. Eighteen years are not enough to change them. It takes a hundred and eight, maybe a hundred and eighty centuries."

On February 26, 1940, Mussolini disappointed American ambassador Sumner Welles, who had gone to Rome to ask Mussolini to volunteer as a negotiator. Il Duce refused.

Welles went home to Washington, D.C., with little hope for peace and with a poor impression of Il Duce's health.

"He was ponderous and static rather than vital," Welles wrote. "He moved with an elephantine motion; every step appeared an effort. He was heavy for his height, and his face in repose fell in rolls of flesh. His close-cropped hair was snow white."

Mussolini's worries, combined with attacks of indigestion that were growing more and more frequent, had aged him.

England, meanwhile, tightening its blockade of Germany, seized several Italian ships loaded with German coal and other raw materials that Hitler had promised. England ignored Mussolini's protests and left him muttering threats against the Allies. It was in this mood that the visiting Ribbentrop found him on March 10. The German foreign minister arrived with Hitler's four-thousand-word answer to Mussolini's critical letter.

The Fuehrer politely and patiently countered every point Il Duce had made and concluded by saying that when the great fighting begins, "your place will more than ever be at our side, just as mine will be at yours."

Despite the letter's friendly tone, Mussolini was guarded in his first conversations with Ribbentrop. Il Duce even turned down the suggestion of another meeting with Hitler. After a night's sleep, however, Mussolini reversed himself completely. He promised that Italy would soon join the fight, and he agreed to meet Hitler at the Brenner Pass as soon as possible.

What had changed Mussolini's mood? It is impossible to say, but abrupt change was typical of his behavior during this period.

When Sumner Welles returned to Rome to make a final bid for peace, he reported a healthier, more confident Mussolini who "seemed to have thrown off some great weight." Welles, who knew about Ribbentrop's recent visit, correctly guessed that Mussolini had shoved all doubts aside and decided at last to fight at Germany's side.

Ciano and most other advisers continued to urge neutrality, but Il Duce's mind was made up. When he met Hitler at the Italian frontier on March 18 the question was not if, but when, Italy would declare war.

The conference, in Mussolini's train coach, was one-sided as usual. Hitler lectured. Mussolini listened. If Italy was content with a second-rate role in the Mediterranean, Hitler said, it need not fight. But if Italy wanted to be a first-rate power, then it must help destroy England and France. Hitler said he was not asking for help. Germany could win its own battles. He was only offering Il Duce an opportunity to achieve the empire of his dreams.

Mussolini had heard it all before, and when he finally got a chance to speak, he assured the Fuehrer that Italy would fight. He said he would be ready for an offensive war in three months.

Hitler would not agree to a three-month delay, but said it might be wise for Italy to hold off its attack on France until after Germany had routed the French army. Then, if Mussolini could launch an attack, Allied resistance would crumble. This was exactly the strategy Il Duce had wanted but had been afraid to suggest. He cheerfully agreed to invade a defeated France.

Although Hitler did most of the talking, he went home without informing Mussolini that Germany would invade Denmark and Norway before attacking France.

Thus, on April 9, Mussolini once again learned of Nazi invasions after they had begun. Instead of being upset over Hitler's lack of trust, Mussolini thought of the invasions as a reprieve. The campaigns in Norway and Denmark would give him more time to prepare his country for war. He ordered the Fascist press to praise Germany's bold move.

Resistance in Norway and Denmark, however, was practically nonexistent, and the fighting ended a few weeks after it began. By the end of April Germany was ready to attack France. Hermann Goering, Hitler's air minister, promised Mussolini he would be warned of the attack at least two weeks before it began.

The promise was broken in the early hours of May 11 when Il Duce woke to the news that German troops had invaded Holland and Belgium. Again there was no advance notice of any kind, but this time the German ambassador in Rome gave Mussolini a letter from Hitler. Il Duce, the Fuehrer wrote, should do what he thought necessary to benefit Italy.

Mussolini wanted his army to cross Italy's border into France at once, but his generals insisted that Italian troops were not yet ready for such a campaign. Impatiently, Mussolini listened to reports of the rapid German advance across Holland and Belgium and into northern France.

At this point, Winston Churchill, who had become prime minister of England in her hour of crisis, wrote to urge Mussolini's continued neutrality:

> "I beg you to believe that it is in no spirit of weakness or fear that I make this solemn appeal, which will remain on record. Down the ages above all other calls comes the cry that the joint heirs of Latin and Christian civilizations must not be ranged against one another in mortal strife. Hearken to it, I beseech you in all honor and respect, before the dread signal is given. It will never be given by us."

Mussolini was moved by Churchill's sincerity, but the appeal came too late. It and other appeals from France and the United States were brushed aside.

On May 28, Belgium surrendered, and in the few frantic days that followed, England managed to evacuate what remained of its army from the beaches of Dunkirk.

Convinced now that Germany would win, Mussolini, in a long letter to Hitler, announced his intention to invade France on June 5. With little foundation in fact, Il Duce claimed that Italy now had seventy divisions ready to fight and that her army and navy were already on war alert. Hitler, advised not to take Il Duce's claims seriously, nevertheless gleefully wrote back that Mussolini's decision would make a strategic as well as a psychological impact on the enemy.

But there was a hitch. The Luftwaffe, Germany's deadly air force, was about to destroy what remained of French aircraft. If Italy opened a second front, the French might regroup their planes, making the destruction more difficult. Hitler asked that the invasion of southern France be delayed briefly. Mussolini reluctantly rescheduled his attack for June 11, 1940.

He told the king of his decision, but Mussolini did not consult Parliament or the grand council of the Fascist party. Even after he had set the date for war, Mussolini deliberately misled some council members. Thus, his decision took most government officials by surprise. He responded confidently to all protests by saying that the war was his responsibility.

On June 10, Ciano summoned both the British and French ambassadors to inform them of Il Duce's intentions. The British ambassador walked out without saying a word, but the French ambassador left the room with a warning: "The Germans are hard masters. You, too, will learn this."

That evening, speaking from the balcony of the Palazzo Venezia, Il Duce told the people crowding the square below that in an "hour marked by destiny" Italy was joining the fight "against the plutocratic and reactionary democracies of the West, who have always hindered the advance and have often plotted against the very existence of the Italian people."

Although the crowd cheered his speech, Mussolini was

never able to generate much public enthusiasm for war or for an alliance with Germany.

Mussolini's own enthusiasm, however, was at first boundless. It blinded him to Italy's secondary role in Hitler's game. Mussolini believed, or at least pretended to believe, that Italy was an equal partner in the Axis. While Germany would win victories in the north, Italy would win victories in the south. There was no need to coordinate military strategy.

Actually, Hitler expected independent Italian operations the moment Il Duce declared war. But June 11 passed with no reports of action. The next day was also quiet, and the next. Malta, England's island stronghold in the center of the Mediterranean, was not attacked or even blockaded. French Tunisia, sharing a border with Italian Libya, was not invaded. Even the French-Italian border remained quiet.

On June 14, 1940, German troops captured Paris. The Italians still had done nothing, but on June 15 Mussolini told Marshal Pietro Badoglio, the hero of Abyssinia, to invade France on June 18.

Badoglio asked for a delay. He was not worried about opposition. The French army was by now defeated. The French government was about to surrender. The problem, Badoglio said, was poor communication. It would take twenty-five days to deploy the army for an attack. Mussolini, however, insisted that the invasion begin on June 18. He sent Badoglio a special division from the Po Valley. The division did nothing but jam the border rail lines, already crowded with one-way traffic. Badoglio did manage to launch a feeble attack on the eighteenth. In four days the Italian army captured two small French towns and bogged to a halt in the streets of a third.

It was a humiliated Mussolini who attended the armistice conference in Munich. He had little hope of getting anything from defeated France, but he was not shy about asking. Italy, he said, wanted to occupy southern France and see French Tunisia disarmed. Hitler refused both requests.

Although he did not tell Mussolini, Hitler now wanted to invade Russia. To do this he had to neutralize the West by negotiating peace with England and giving France a truce that was mild enough to discourage further resistance. Letting the French keep southern France and Tunisia was thus part of Hitler's political strategy. Il Duce, unaware of the strategy, returned to Rome feeling betrayed.

Weeks of uncertainty and inaction followed the French truce. Mussolini offered to participate in the invasion of England. Hitler declined the offer without explaining that he hoped to make peace.

On July 19 Hitler made a formal appeal to England for peace. It was rejected immediately, and Hitler realized he must change his plans. Before invading Russia, he must destroy England. Russia, however, was already causing trouble in the Balkans. The prize there was the Rumanian oil, and oil was vital to Hitler's war plans. He could only hope that Russia would continue to move cautiously. He advised Mussolini to do nothing to upset the uneasy balance of power in the Balkans.

Mussolini, however, was growing impatient. Italy had been at war for two months with nothing to show for it, and so he began making plans to invade Yugoslavia, Greece, or Egypt. Hitler had once recommended the invasion of Yugoslavia, that and the invasion of Greece were now the two things he least wanted from Italy. He had not, however, fully explained his plans to Mussolini.

Il Duce went on preparing various campaigns until September 13 when his desert army in Libya, after much prodding, finally crossed the border into Egypt. Although England's desert army gave ground slowly against the invaders, Sidi Barrini, sixty miles inside Egypt, fell to the Italians after just four days of fighting. The advance stopped there, but Mussolini was delighted.

His pleasure, however, did not last.

17

Hard Realities

THE YEAR 1940 began well for the Axis. Italian forces, still inside Egypt, threatened England's last North African foothold. The German army stood at the western edge of the European continent, threatening England itself. As the year advanced, however, Germany and Italy began to suffer reverses that forced Hitler and Mussolini to face some hard realities.

For Hitler, the toughest reality to accept was that England, despite its hopeless position, would not make peace. Its army had barely escaped destruction at Dunkirk. Its air force was reduced to a few planes. Its major cities were being bombed to rubble. But instead of faltering as Hitler expected, England only grew more determined to fight on.

Germany prepared for Operation Sea Lion, code name for the invasion of England. Hitler, meanwhile, offered again and again to negotiate a treaty. England refused again and again.

France also disappointed Hitler. The Vichy government he had set up to rule occupied France was supposed to join the fight against England, and Vichy indeed had promised to declare war. But the promise was never kept. It seemed that the only Frenchmen willing to fight were those who had escaped from France to join Charles de Gaulle's overseas army. de Gaulle had vowed to fight until France was free once again.

Spain also disappointed the Axis. Franco, ruling a country

145

that still had not recovered from its terrible civil war, was determined to remain neutral. Hitler tried hard to change Franco's position. At one point the Fuehrer offered to take Gibraltar, the English fortress at the southern tip of Spain that guarded the entrance to the Mediterranean. Hitler thought that taking it with German troops and giving Gibraltar to Spain would be tempting bait, but the offer wounded Franco's pride. He replied icily that if the fortress were to be taken it would be taken by Spanish troops.

Mussolini, in his dealings with Hitler, also had to stomach a hard reality. Italy's role in the Axis partnership would always be secondary. It hurt his pride when Hitler refused his offer of Italian troops for Operation Sea Lion. And when Mussolini announced that Italy was preparing to take Yugoslavia, Hitler ordered him to cancel the invasion and sent a long letter patiently explaining the Balkan situation. It seemed that Italy could do nothing without Hitler's approval.

Later, of course, Yugoslavia was invaded and occupied, but it was a German, not an Italian, operation. Meanwhile, Hitler told Mussolini to put every effort into forcing the British out of Africa. This raised another uncomfortable reality. The Italian army in Egypt would not or could not advance, and Italian garrisons in Abyssinia, Eritrea, and Somaliland were crumbling under British attack.

In the summer of 1940, Hitler added to Axis problems by making a huge tactical error. To prepare for the invasion of England, the Luftwaffe had been steadily destroying the Royal Air Force. Gallant British pilots, flying Spitfires, perhaps the best fighter plane of the day, gave the Germans a tough fight, but time and superior numbers were on Germany's side. But just when the air battle seemed over, Hitler changed his strategy.

Instead of bombing airfields and searching for British planes, he ordered the Luftwaffe to begin large-scale bombing of British cities. He hoped to break the English will, but he hoped in vain. Although the bombing took a terrible toll of life and property, it only strengthened the resolve of the British people to fight on. Meanwhile, the RAF had been given time to start rebuilding.

Hitler, beginning to have doubts about Operation Sea Lion, was more and more troubled by reports from the Balkans. Using political pressure and military threats, Russia was gradually extending its influence toward the Rumanian oil fields. If not stopped, Russia would eventually control all the Balkan countries. Under heavy secrecy, Hitler told his generals to speed up their plans for the invasion of Russia. Mussolini, of course, was not consulted. In fact, Hitler encouraged Mussolini to believe that the nonaggression pact with Russia would preserve peace in the east for years to come.

Even Stalin, the crafty Russian dictator, knew better. He looked on the pact as little more than a license for Russia to grab what territory it could in the Balkans. And he knew if he moved too fast or too far, the license would expire.

Mussolini jumped into this delicate situation with both clumsy feet. In the bliss of ignorance and restless from inactivity and injured pride, Mussolini decided in the fall of 1940 that the time had come for Italy to invade Greece.

He launched the campaign without telling Hitler. If warned in advance, Hitler might have ordered a humiliating cancellation, as he had done with Yugoslavia. And by keeping his plans to himself, Mussolini was taking a page from Hitler's book. Mussolini, after all, had learned about Hitler's ventures only after they had begun.

The invasion began in the early hours of October 28, 1940, when Italian troops crossed the Albanian border into Greece.

Hitler, who had just had another unsuccessful meeting with Franco, was on his way to Florence to confer with Il Duce. He learned of the Greek invasion when he was greeted at the Florence railroad station.

A jubilant Mussolini announced: "Victorious Italian troops crossed the Greco-Albanian frontier at dawn today!"

Hitler, surprised and angry, could hardly speak. He uttered a few coldly polite words and led the way from the railroad station. A few minutes later, when the conference began, Hitler still did not trust himself to speak about the latest Italian venture. Instead, he gave a falsely optimistic report on his meeting with Franco. Spain, Hitler suggested, would soon join the Axis.

Later, Hitler questioned the wisdom of invading Greece at the start of winter and marveled that the Italian army, which he thought needed better equipment and more training, had been brought to fighting trim so quickly. He also expressed the hope that Stalin would not use the invasion as an excuse to advance on the Rumanian oil fields.

By the time Hitler said good-bye, Mussolini had lost his jubilance.

The invasion of Greece touched off a series of Italian disasters. It took Greek soldiers just a few days to put the Italians in retreat along the Albanian front.

The British navy reacted to the invasion by occupying several islands in the Aegean Sea and intensifying its search for Italian warships. The Italian navy was not prepared for battle.

On November 11, a British task force caught the main Italian fleet anchored in Taranto harbor at the southern end of Italy. When the shelling ended, one Italian battleship lay at the bottom of the harbor. Two others were seriously damaged, and the dockyards were a smoking ruin. In just a few minutes of battle, Italy lost control of the Mediterranean.

Mussolini needed help at once. Early in December 1940 he sent a special ambassador to Berlin to ask for aid. After scolding the ambassador on Italy's poor strategy and poor performance, Hitler agreed to send a small fleet of German transport planes, which were of little use at the moment.

Mussolini had hardly recovered from this humiliation when he received devastating news from Egypt. The British, on December 9, 1940, launched a massive offensive that caught the Italian desert army completely off guard.

Il Duce was stunned, and the news grew worse. The British chased Italy out of Egypt and captured Tobruk, in Libya. By January 7, Italy had lost more than seven hundred pieces of artillery, and the British held 113,000 Italian prisoners.

Could Germany, Mussolini asked, send help to North Africa? Hitler answered that help would be given only on the condition that Mussolini recruit Italian men by the thousands and send them to Germany to work in fields and factories. It was a crushing answer, but Mussolini had no choice.

The early days of 1941 brought further humiliation from Hitler. Still thinking of Russia as an Axis ally, Mussolini had begun discussing a mutual assistance pact with the Soviet ambassador in Rome. Il Duce's naive hope was that Russia might supply some of the raw materials that Italy needed. The talks were proceeding well until Hitler learned about them. He ordered Mussolini to break off discussions at once. Il Duce complied without asking for an explanation.

Mussolini might have guessed what was coming when Hitler told him soon after the new year began that the invasion of Britain would be delayed in order to concentrate German forces in the east. Hitler said, however, that the shift was needed for the spring invasion of Greece and Yugoslavia. He did not mention Russia. Mussolini was asked to regain the offensive on the Albanian frontier and try to persuade Franco to join the Axis.

At the moment, Mussolini was not the most enthusiastic salesman for alliance, but he agreed to meet Franco on February 12 at Bordighera, a coastal town in northwest Italy. Franco arrived with many arguments for Spanish neutrality. Mussolini agreed with all of them, and a surprised Franco returned to Spain more determined than ever to stay out of the war.

Back in Rome, the news was grim. The British desert army was still advancing into Libya. Italy's East African colonies were almost entirely in British hands. The Albanian frontier was stabilized, but as soon as the snow melted, the Greeks were sure to take the offensive.

In sharp contrast, the German army rose to new glory. On April 6, German troops, having crossed Bulgaria by treaty, invaded Greece and Yugoslavia with dazzling speed. Belgrade, the capital of Yugoslavia, fell within a week. On April 23, the Greek army surrendered. A British expeditionary force of fifty thousand troops barely escaped from the Greek mainland. German workers in Greece began building airfields that would put the Luftwaffe in bomber range of North Africa.

Meanwhile, on the ground in North Africa, Marshal Erwin Rommel, Germany's most brilliant and daring strategist, slashed into the British. In just twelve days Rommel drove the British out of Libya to defensive lines well inside Egypt. Had the all-out assault continued, the British might have been forced out of Egypt entirely, but Hitler halted the attack. He needed all the units he could spare for the invasion of Russia, which had to begin while the summer was still young.

Nazi U-boats won further glory. They sank so many Allied ships that it seemed certain that England, cut off from supplies, would soon beg for peace. England's only success during this period was the sinking of the German battleship *Bismarck.*

By June of 1941 it was obvious to almost everyone that Germany was about to invade Russia. The Allies suspected it. Even Stalin guessed that German troops had not gathered on his border for training exercises. Mussolini, however, remained ignorant.

Then, at 3 A.M., June 22, a German diplomat in Rome woke Ciano with a telephone report. German troops a few hours earlier had crossed the border into Russia. Mussolini offered at once to send Italian troops to assist in the invasion. Hitler, now painfully aware of the Italian army's record, accepted the troops with great reluctance.

The German army enjoyed early success on all sectors of the vast Russian front. Complete victory was predicted in a matter of weeks. A confident Hitler asked Mussolini to join in a tour of the front on August 25, 1941.

The invitation came at a tragic time for Mussolini and his family. On August 7, Bruno Mussolini, eighteen, the second son and Il Duce's favorite, was killed when a new bomber he was testing crashed near Pisa. There was an engine failure soon after takeoff. Two crewmen survived, but Bruno did not. Mussolini still suffered from the initial shock of this loss when he joined Hitler in Russia.

Hitler, too sated with success to offer much sympathy or understanding, bluntly refused Il Duce's offer of more Italian troops.

Later, Mussolini and Hitler drafted a press release that spoke of a "New Order" for Europe, a phrase that would be used often in future Nazi propaganda to describe the era of "prosperity and justice" promised after the war ended.

By now, however, Il Duce had grown skeptical. And soon after returning to Rome he received reports of suffering among Italian workers who had been sent to Germany. Their camps were no better than prisons. The men were ill-fed and beaten regularly. Escapees were hunted down with vicious dogs.

Mussolini complained angrily to Hitler. The Fuehrer told Mussolini not to be misled by enemy propaganda.

But it was not propaganda. Mussolini also learned that thousands of Greeks were starving, and that captured Russians were so tormented by hunger that cannibalism had broken out in Nazi prison camps. It was predicted that twenty to thirty million Russians citizens would die of hunger before the year ended.

It seemed that the "prosperity and justice" of the "New Order" had not yet arrived.

Meanwhile, the situation in North Africa changed again. In an offensive launched November 18, the British drove Rommel out of Egypt and overran Tobruk on November 29. Rommel, who lost thirty-three thousand men, ordered a general retreat.

Still in low spirits over these battle reports, Mussolini was surprised on December 3, 1941, when the Japanese ambassador told him war between Japan and the United States was likely to start at any moment. The ambassador expected Italy and Germany to join in the fight against America.

Mussolini cheerfully assured the ambassador that Italy would welcome a war on two continents. Il Duce may have thought Italy would gain a more important military role in an expanded struggle. Or perhaps he was just curious to see how Hitler would deal with a new, powerful enemy.

On December 7 Japanese planes caught the U.S. Pacific Fleet in Pearl Harbor. The surprise attack with bombs and torpedoes left many ships sinking or severely damaged. The United States promptly declared war on Japan, Germany, and Italy.

Mussolini was jubilant when he spoke from the balcony of the Palazzo Venezia on December 11, saying that the United States had been added to Italy's list of enemies. In Germany, Hitler made a similar public declaration, but at the moment all his attention was on the Russian front where the German army had run into serious trouble.

18

Flawed Alliance

HITLER'S ARMIES were not prepared for the terrible Russian winter. The men suffered hunger, disease, and the tortures of sub-zero cold, and on December 6, long after snow and ice had halted the German tanks and other armored units, the Russians launched an unexpected counterattack.

It was fierce. A tactical retreat might have saved many German lives, but the Fuehrer would not allow retreat. Just the same, his army was forced to give ground, but the cost in suffering, injury, and death was tragic.

Most Italians were now anti-German. Not only were Italian laborers in Germany treated little better than slaves, but the German military advisers now coming into Italy in increasing numbers regarded Italians as second-rate citizens.

In North Africa, German and Italian troops could not cooperate. Rommel refused to give Italians anything but minor assignments in his campaigns. German convoys would not even let Italian troops share the road. Italian officers on important missions had to wait at the sides of dusty roads to let German troops pass. And the Germans, of course, blamed the Italians for all the problems in North Africa.

Although eager to see the arrogant Germans humbled, Mussolini still believed in eventual victory for the Axis, a victory that would benefit Italy only if Italians did their part. For this

153

reason, contrary to all advice, he ordered more Italian troops to the Russian front.

He should have concentrated all available manpower in North Africa. By mid-December the British advance threatened to clear the entire coast of Libya. Axis field generals, including Rommel himself, said it might be necessary to retreat into Tunisia simply to save what remained of the army. Hitler, however, refused to allow it. Tunisia, long a French colony, was now ruled by Vichy, and Hitler still hoped for military support from Vichy. Violating Tunisia's border would erase all hope of it.

It often seemed that Hitler was more concerned about Vichy than about Italy. High-ranking Fascists, even members of the grand council, openly criticized Il Duce and his pro-German policies. Even Ciano spoke against the conduct of the war. And Ciano was also heard berating his father-in-law for the affair with Clara Petacci. When friends reminded Ciano that he himself was no model of fidelity, he answered that brief affairs could be forgiven but the long-lasting Petacci affair was a scandal.

As morale sagged, the Fascist party lost power. For too long Il Duce had acted without consulting party leaders. Although the party's grand council still met, its function was to rubber-stamp decisions Mussolini had already made. Gradually, however, individual members of the council began asking each other what could be done to save Italy. This question grew in importance daily as Axis fortunes worsened.

Early in 1942 Hitler sent Hermann Goering to Rome to bolster Italian spirits. His visit was a diplomatic disaster. The field marshal's gluttony and endless boasting about his art and jewelry collections offended Italian sensibilities. The full-length sable coat that the fat German sported everywhere was in bad taste to fashion-conscious Romans. One critic said such a garment might be worn by an expensive prostitute attending the opera, but on no other person or occasion would it be appropriate.

Late in April Hitler summoned Mussolini and Ciano to

Germany for another conference. The Fuehrer wanted to strengthen Italian resolve. As usual, Hitler did all the talking, but Mussolini did indeed return to Rome in better spirits. And in May good news came from North Africa. Rommel had launched a brutal counterattack. It was a great success.

The British retreated across the all-too-familiar African desert. On June 21, 1942, Tobruk once again fell into Axis hands. Rommel captured thirty-three thousand British soldiers and enough gasoline and other stores to supply his own army for three months. With the road to Egypt now apparently open at last, Mussolini flew across the Mediterranean to share the glory with his troops. His arrival in North Africa on June 29 was marked with tragedy when the second plane in his entourage crashed, killing several aides.

Italian generals greeted Il Duce with long faces and reports that the advance was stalled at Alamein, some two hundred miles west of Cairo. Mussolini assumed the halt was only temporary, but nothing happened. For three weeks he waited behind the lines for the advance to resume. He expected a visit from Rommel but the "Desert Fox," as he had become known, never paid his respects to the Italian dictator. During this time Hitler added to the insult by promoting Rommel to marshal, a rank above any of the Italian field generals.

Trying to hide his displeasure, Mussolini kept busy making optimistic plans for Egypt. He proposed that Germany rule the military while Italy ruled the civil government. But his plans for governing Egypt proved to be fantasy.

When he finally left North Africa, the front was still stagnant. Hope of swift conquest had died. The Axis would never take the offensive again in North Africa.

He stopped in Athens on his way home and was shocked at the starvation and poverty. In a long and compassionate message to Hitler, Mussolini described the situation and pleaded for Greek aid. Hitler answered bluntly that the Greeks would have to fend for themselves.

Mussolini was infuriated. By the time he reached Rome, he was physically ill. Wave after wave of stomach pains left him gasping. Doctors believed that an acute case of dysentery had reactivated an old ulcer, but worry certainly contributed to Mussolini's physical problems. Doctors could find no remedy. Meanwhile, Mussolini's robust frame shrunk by forty pounds. Pain pills helped, but there were many days when he was in too much agony to work.

The war went badly. Sea convoys trying to supply the desert army were under constant attack. Sunken Italian ships could not be replaced. Only half the vital gasoline loaded at Italian ports reached Rommel's army. Just the same, on August 30, Rommel tried to resume his offensive. His attack failed. Two months later, the British began a relentless offensive to push the Germans back. And on November 7, 1942, far to the west, Allied forces landed in Morocco and Algeria. Rommel, now caught between two armies, knew the desert had been lost.

Hitler, however, would not give up. He called for an immediate conference with Mussolini. Il Duce was too sick to travel, but Ciano went to Germany and heard the Fuehrer outline plans for an Axis landing in Tunisia. Ciano thought reinforcing Rommel should be the first priority. He could see no tactical importance in Tunisia, particularly when Vichy France refused to cooperate. But it was useless to argue. Hitler had made up his mind.

The first German units landed at Tunis, the major city of Tunisia, on November 11. They were followed by 250,000 German and Italian troops. They did little to stop the advance of superior Allied forces, and supplying the beachhead put further strain on Italian shipping.

Meanwhile, the Fuehrer impulsively ordered German and Italian troops into Vichy-controlled southern France. The French retaliated at the port of Toulon where they scuttled the navy that Hitler had long coveted for his own use. Sixteen submarines, twenty-nine destroyers and torpedo boats, seven cruisers, two battle cruisers, and one battleship sank to the bottom of Toulon harbor.

Defeat was in the air. Hitler again sent Goering to Rome to bolster morale. Again, the field marshal achieved nothing. Hitler next called another Axis conference. Mussolini, still sick, again sent Ciano to Germany. This time, Ciano arrived in Germany on December 18 with instructions to urge peace between Germany and Russia.

He found German military headquarters in deep gloom over a steady flow of bad news from the Russian front. The German Sixth Army was isolated near Stalingrad. All attempts to relieve it failed. It seemed like a good climate to talk peace, but Hitler refused to consider Ciano's recommendation.

Back in Italy, Ciano could find nothing to restore hope. Allied planes had begun bombing Italian cities. There was a shortage of food. Mussolini was too sick to provide any leadership.

Peace was the major topic, but it often led to argument. Although most members of the Fascist grand council wanted peace, few could agree on how to achieve it. Some thought peace possible only under Mussolini's leadership. Others, the party dissidents, thought Mussolini would have to step down before peace could be negotiated.

Ciano sided with the dissidents and was even seen lunching with two council dissidents who wanted Italy to break her alliance with Germany. Nothing was decided, partly because Mussolini was too sick to call a meeting of the council.

He spent Christmas of 1942 in bed. For a time his doctors thought he had cancer of the stomach. Later, however, it seemed he was suffering from an acute gastric ulcer. In any case, standard ulcer treatment brought gradual improvement in Il Duce's health.

On January 23, 1943, he was well enough to attend a meeting of his cabinet, and on February 5, in an attempt to silent dissidents, he reorganized his government. Nearly all cabinet members were replaced or reassigned. Even Ciano was shifted from foreign minister to ambassador to the Vatican. Henceforth, Il Duce himself would head the foreign office.

The changes, done as usual without any advance notice to those involved, did nothing to lift morale. On March 6, strikes halted production at several key munitions plants. Threats got some production started again, but many plants remained idle for several days. Work was not resumed at the giant Fiat factory until a 300-lire bonus was promised to each man.

Hitler, fully informed of Italy's crumbling resolve, once again summoned Mussolini to Germany. This time, Il Duce thought he was well enough to travel, but soon after boarding the train on April 6 he suffered a renewed attack of pain. He had intended to insist on a separate peace with Russia, but when the conference began he was still too sick to argue. In any case, Hitler stated that Nazi victory in the east remained the first priority. Even though Italy was threatened, the southern front would hold secondary importance in Hitler's strategy.

Despite Hitler's stubborn position and his own stomach pains, Mussolini returned to Rome in improved spirits. Again some of Hitler's confidence and optimism had rubbed off on him.

In Rome, however, Il Duce faced more trouble. Criticism of the war, the Germans, and the Fuehrer could be heard everywhere. It now seemed certain that the Axis would lose Tunisia. Mussolini was reluctant to ask for more help from Germany, but by April 30, the situation was desperate. In an urgent message, Il Duce told the Fuehrer that without air reinforcements, Tunisia would be lost.

Hitler did not respond to the message. Unknown to Mussolini, the Fuehrer had already decided to write off Tunisia and the hastily organized army he had sent there.

In Rome, the Fascist dissidents gained strength. Plotting Mussolini's overthrow was their main concern. Some of the plots were reported to him. He responded with the dramatic oratory that had once served him so well. On May 3, he spoke to party leaders, appealing for a strengthening of national resistance, and on May 5, the seventh anniversary of victory in Abyssinia, he addressed the public from the balcony of the Palazzo Venezia for the last time.

"The bloody sacrifices of these hard times," he declared, "will be recompensed by victory. . . . "

The crowd cheered wildly, but there were no victories.

Eight days after the speech, the remnants of the Axis army in Tunisia surrendered.

At last, Hitler seemed to recognize the danger on his southern front and decided to keep the war there as far from the German homeland as possible. He offered Mussolini five German divisions to defend Italy. To Hitler's surprise, Mussolini refused the offer. Il Duce could not admit he needed help.

Hitler ordered his generals to start planning a German defense of Italy anyway. He knew by now that Mussolini was in danger of losing control of the government. If the dissidents gained power and made a separate peace with the Allies, Germany must be ready to defend Italy alone.

On May 30 Mussolini suffered the most painful attack yet. He thought he was dying.

At this point the king began playing a role in the dissident plot. He could no longer rely on a man who had not only lost the people's trust but was also too sick to govern.

The king desperately wanted peace. In a memorandum setting forth his position, he wrote: "One must think seriously of the possible need to detach Italy's armed forces from those of Germany. . . ."

Later, after meeting with politicians from the pre-Fascist era and with dissidents in the present government, he told Dino Grandi, the dissident former Minister of Justice, to be patient: "The moment will come. I know that I can count on you. Let your king choose the opportune moment and in the meantime help me obtain the constitutional means."

The king, always a strong advocate of constitutional law, wanted a vote from the grand council or the Chamber of Deputies to endorse any change he might make in the government. He also feared Hitler's revenge. If Mussolini were deposed, German soldiers might be turned loose to ravage Italian citizens and property.

For several weeks, the king thought it might be necessary to keep Mussolini at some position in the government simply to keep Hitler from unleashing his rage.

On July 9, 1943, the Allies landed in Sicily. The few German units on the island put up strong resistance. Most of the Italian defenders, however, would not fight. The admiral in charge of the main Italian naval base blew up his guns and surrendered without firing a shell. In most towns the civilians welcomed the arrival of the Allied troops.

On July 12, Mussolini's request for German air support was answered with insult. If the Italians would not fight, the Fuehrer said, he would not send any more military aid.

Soon after, fourteen loyal Fascists confronted Mussolini with a proposal. These were men who had agreed to make speeches throughout the country to bolster morale. They told Mussolini he should change his style of government. If he gave up personal control in favor of control by the grand council or the chamber, they argued, he could ease his responsibilities and worries. Although the men all had sincere intentions, Mussolini treated their suggestion with suspicion. But he did agree to call a meeting of the grand council to discuss their suggestion.

Hitler, meanwhile, asked for yet another meeting with Mussolini. It was held July 19 in a villa near Venice. Although there was little time to prepare for the session, Mussolini's advisers urged him to demand that Italy either be granted full military assistance or else be released from the war. Il Duce promised to make this demand, but he knew that once facing Hitler, he was not likely to do it.

Indeed, Hitler opened the session by talking nonstop for

two hours. At noon, he was interrupted by the entry of a secretary who informed Mussolini that Rome at the moment was under violent bombardment by Allied planes.

Mussolini was stunned, but when the secretary left, Hitler went right on talking without a word of commiseration. It was a depressing meeting. Hitler scolded and harangued. His endless flow of words were not translated, so Il Duce's aides had little idea of what was being said. They simply waited vainly for Mussolini to state Italy's case.

The Fuehrer covered the whole range of his creed. He stated again that Russia must be defeated. He promised that England would be brought to its knees by submarine attack and a new secret weapon (recently developed guided missiles). And he said Italy would get no further German military aid until Italian soldiers decided to fight. If Germany were given full military control of Italy's defense, however, Hitler said, assistance would be provided.

When the meeting ended, Mussolini told his aides that Hitler had promised to send help, but he did not explain the conditions.

The conspirators, who saw that nothing was gained in the meeting with Hitler, agreed that the time had come to act. To save Italy, Mussolini must be removed from office.

19

Arrest

MUSSOLINI'S JULY 19 meeting with Hitler had been the last hope for Italian fascism. When Il Duce failed to make clear that Italy would not continue fighting without immediate military aid, support for Dino Grandi and the other dissidents came from all quarters of government. The king was ready to act.

Had Mussolini not been so occupied with the bombing of Rome and the rapid advance of the Allies in Sicily he might have recognized the obvious danger signs. He was not even alarmed when Grandi openly circulated a motion that he planned to present at the July 24 meeting of the grand council. It called for reviving the powers of the cabinet, the Parliament, and the corporations, and giving the king command of the armed forces.

To avoid charges of conspiracy, Grandi showed the motion to everyone, including Mussolini. Although Mussolini described it as "inadmissible and contemptible," he did not seem to see it as a serious threat to his regime.

The Germans were also blind to the pending crisis. Four days before the council met, the German ambassador in Rome told Hitler that Grandi's proposals would free Mussolini of civil responsibilities and give him more time for the war effort.

Had the ambassador known what was happening at the palace he would have been alarmed. The king had assumed an active role at last in his country's destiny. Sure that Grandi's motion would pass, Victor Emmanuel and his advisers were hard at work organizing a new government. Their plans included the arrest of Mussolini and the appointment of Marshal Pietro Badoglio, the hero of the Abyssinian war, as the new prime minister.

Although the king worked in strict secrecy, rumors from the palace reached Mussolini's friends. They warned him and urged the immediate arrest of the dissidents. Rachele, who had never trusted politicians, told her husband to either arrest Grandi and his supporters or else cancel the meeting of the grand council.

Mussolini answered all warnings by saying that the king had always supported him and was too close a friend to plot against him.

Perhaps, in good health, Mussolini's instincts would have warned him, but stomach pains continued to drain his energy and dull his mind. He later wrote of this period that he could see clearly what was happening but lacked the energy or the interest to resist.

On July 22, after making an appointment, Grandi met Mussolini privately at Palazzo Venezia to discuss the motion. There are conflicting reports on what happened, but Grandi later said he told Il Duce that the only responsible thing to do was resign and give the Italian people a chance to form a new government. Grandi argued that the war was lost, but if Il Duce resigned now, the wrath of the Allies would fall on fascism and not on the Italian nation itself.

Grandi reported that Mussolini listened affably and agreed that it would be proper to step down if the war actually were lost. But the fact was, Mussolini declared, that the war was soon to be won by a German secret weapon that would reverse the military situation completely.

Aides listening outside the office claimed that Mussolini was anything but affable and was heard to rage at Grandi. In any case, nothing was accomplished by the meeting.

As the fateful July 24, a Saturday, approached, Mussolini decided he would let each member of the grand council speak. This, he thought, would clear the air and allow the regime to move forward with positive support. His plan, however, made it necessary to extend the time for the meeting. Thus it was decided to convene at 5 P.M. instead of the usual 10 P.M.

As the members gathered at the Palazzo Venezia, Grandi and his followers grew more and more nervous. A larger than normal force of Fascist militia in the courtyard and hallways hardly had a calming effect. It seemed certain to many dissidents that they would be arrested after or perhaps even during the session.

But the meeting began without incident. Mussolini, in the colorful uniform of a militia officer, took his seat on the raised dais at the head of the table and, as usual, opened the discussion with his own statement.

It was rambling, poorly organized, and long. Although he defended past actions, he spoke without spirit or confidence. His candor was surprising. "At this moment," he said, "I am certainly the most disliked or, rather, loathed man in Italy."

He blamed most of the country's problems on the military conduct of the war. He admitted that he was ultimately responsible as supreme commander of the armed forces, but declared that he had never wanted this job. He put no blame on Germany for withholding promised aid. Instead, he listed all the arms and materials Germany had sent and praised German generosity.

He concluded by warning that Grandi's motion could place fascism in jeopardy because it would force the king to choose between continuing the regime or liquidating it entirely.

His speech lasted two hours.

He was followed by de Bono and de Vecchi, two surviving members of the quadrumvirate. Each spoke briefly in defense of the army.

Grandi rose next to deliver his challenge. He blamed the dictatorship, not the army, for Italy's problems. He said that the nation had been betrayed on the day it had been allied with Germany. After reading the terms of his motion, Grandi next attacked Mussolini's system of personal rule, blaming him for the war and for fascism's loss of popular support.

After an hour of talk, Grandi gave way to other members who spoke either for or against the motion. Ciano sided with Grandi.

Mussolini showed little emotion. He sat like a judge at a trial. Occasionally, pain forced him to grimace or shield his eyes with a hand.

At midnight, he was exhausted and ordered a fifteen-minute recess. He went to his office, where he drank a glass of milk and spooned raw sugar into his mouth. He needed quick energy to continue the ordeal.

The debate resumed and continued until 2:30 in the morning, when the motion was at last put to the vote. Nineteen voted for it. Seven opposed it. One abstained.

Mussolini rose wearily.

"You have provoked the crisis of the regime," he said. "The session is closed."

It had lasted nearly ten hours. He arrived exhausted at the Villa Torlonia at three o'clock Sunday morning. Rachele, who had been waiting up all night, ran out to meet him. His haggard face told her everything.

"You've had them all arrested, I suppose?" she said.

"No," Mussolini answered. "But I will."

Il Duce, however, was too tired to fight. Perhaps he realized he could do nothing to save Italy. Perhaps a change was really needed. He would arrest no one.

Activity at the palace began early next morning. Soon after sunrise Marshal Badoglio accepted the royal decree appointing him prime minister. Through most of that hot and humid Sunday in July, Italy thus had two prime ministers, but few people knew it.

During the early hours the king and his aides vainly tried

to guess how Mussolini might react to the vote of the grand council. As it turned out, Il Duce decided to act as if nothing unusual had happened. He slept badly and woke early. When his doctor arrived to give him the daily injection for his ulcer, Mussolini refused it, saying his blood was too agitated. Then, following a twenty-one-year habit, he ordered his car to drive him to the Palazzo Venezia.

He arrived at his office at about 9 A.M. and began routinely going through reports and holding interviews. He tried to reach Grandi on the telephone, but was told that Grandi had gone to the country. Shortly before noon, after hearing a report from the ministry of the interior, Mussolini asked an aide to make an appointment with the king for five o'clock that afternoon. Apparently, Mussolini had hoped to take Grandi with him to the palace. But it now seemed that he must go alone.

At noon, Mussolini received a courtesy call from the newly appointed Japanese ambassador. Il Duce turned on all his charm and gave full and candid answers to the ambassador's questions about the military situation in Europe.

The interview apparently restored some of Mussolini's confidence. On his way home for lunch, he had his driver take him to the San Lorenzo area of Rome, which had suffered severe damage in the July 19 bombing. There he left his car, talked to citizens, and took notes. Contact with the people made him even more confident. At home, over a light lunch, he spoke hopefully of his audience with the king. He was certain that the king would find some way, despite Grandi's motion, to save the Fascist regime.

Rachele had doubts. She had never trusted the king, and when she learned that Mussolini had been asked not to wear a uniform but appear at the palace in civilian clothes, she knew the end was near. She told Mussolini that he would not return from the interview.

Mussolini shook his head. The king had supported him for twenty-one years. He was a friend.

Rachele, however, was right. The "friend" had prepared a trap for Il Duce. Police officers hid in an ambulance parked near the palace gate. Fifty policemen waited behind the palace. When he arrived for the appointment, however, Mussolini noticed nothing unusual except that he was a few minutes early. This was just as well because he had a great deal to say to the king.

He planned to downgrade the importance of the crisis by reminding the king that the grand council had no constitutional powers. Its recommendations were merely advisory. He would also report that one member who had voted for Grandi's motion had written a letter in the morning retracting his vote. Mussolini was sure others would want to retract also.

When he stood before the king, however, Mussolini had difficulty remaining calm. His hands shook. His confidence left him. He did mention the council's lack of authority, but before long, the king took charge of the conversation.

He told Mussolini that Italy was defeated, that the army would not fight, and that it would be useless to continue. The king told Mussolini he was the most hated man in the country. He had but one friend left, the king himself, who stood ready to protect him.

King Victor Emmanuel III then asked for Benito Mussolini's resignation. Il Duce was stunned.

"I am sorry," said the king. "I am sorry, but the solution could not have been otherwise."

The king then showed Mussolini to the door, shook his hand, and ended the interview. Il Duce walked from the palace in a daze.

During the meeting, his driver had been taken temporarily into custody. And before Mussolini could begin walking toward his car, he was stopped by two police officers.

One of them said, "His Majesty has charged me with the protection of your person."

Mussolini replied that this was unnecessary and stepped toward his car.

"No, Excellency, you must come in my car." The officer pointed to the ambulance that had been backed up close to the front door of the palace.

Making no further protest, Mussolini followed the officers. One of them supported his elbow as he stepped into the ambulance. Three plainclothes policemen and three others in uniform then crowded into the vehicle.

The doors were closed and the ambulance sped away. Few Romans out on that hot afternoon paid much attention to the ambulance that seemed to be hurrying back from a routine call. There was no way of knowing that the large van with the red crosses carried the most hated man in Italy.

20

Rescue

HE WAS FIRST TAKEN to a police barracks and placed under armed guard in the officers' quarters. A few hours later, the guards moved him to a nearby police academy, which was believed easier to defend. There Mussolini spent the night of July 25.

A doctor visited him. Although Mussolini refused medical attention, he chatted with the doctor about Italy's current dilemma. He seemed in good spirits, but after the doctor left and after Il Duce noticed the sentries outside his door, he began to doubt that the king was interested only in his safety.

Actually, more than anything else at this time, the king feared that the Fascist militia would rescue Mussolini and reestablish his government. But this could not happen because Mussolini, through his personal dominance of everything, had destroyed his regime's ability to act without him.

Although party secretary Carlo Scorza had the authority to rally the militia from every city and town in the nation, he had taken his orders from Mussolini for so long that he could not act independently. When he heard Mussolini had been arrested, Scorza immediately went into hiding without giving any orders.

Enzo Galbiati, general of the militia, and one of the few who had voted against the Grandi motion, also had the power to call up the militia, but he did nothing. Other party leaders either went into hiding or submitted quietly to arrest. Manilo Morgagni, director of a Fascist news agency, took the most decisive action. He committed suicide.

At 10:45 P.M. Sunday, the Italian radio announced Mussolini's "resignation," Badoglio's appointment as prime minister, and the new government's decision to continue fighting against the Allies. Rescuing Il Duce was of no concern to the excited crowds that filled the streets. The people cheered the news. They tore down Fascist posters and symbols and marched to the palace to hail their king.

The citizens of Rome guessed correctly that the decision to continue fighting was just a bid for time. The new government would make peace the moment it was safe to do so. Meanwhile, it was necessary to keep Hitler from taking vengeance on Italy.

Hitler, however, was not fooled, and the Badoglio government soon realized that any effort to rescue Mussolini would be made, not by the Fascists, but by the Germans.

Mussolini asked through a government messenger that he be allowed to go home to Forli and live out the rest of his life in peace. Badoglio at first agreed to this, but officials in Forli protested. Mussolini was so hated in his home district, they said, that it would be impossible to guarantee his safety.

Thus it was decided to take Mussolini under armed guard to one of the small islands off the coast south of Rome. A convoy arrived at the police academy at 7 P.M. Tuesday, July 27. Mussolini, who still thought he was going to Forli, discovered the change in plans only after he looked through a slit in his van's window shade. Instead of going north, the convoy went south.

At a naval dock in Gaeta, Mussolini was taken aboard a ship and transported to the island of Ponza, some thirty-five miles off the Italian coast. There was a prison on the island, but Mussolini was housed in a small cottage outside the prison walls. Comfort was limited. A water shortage made bathing impossible. Mussolini let his beard grow and the gray stubble on his head sprout. For the first few days, he had no change of clothes. On

Thursday, July 29, he quietly observed his sixtieth birthday. He was not just resigned to his fate. He seemed to welcome it.

Among the reflective notes he wrote at this time, he spoke of his wish to return to Forli to "peacefully await the end of my life, which I hope will come soon."

In another note he said, "When a man and his organism collapse, the fall is irretrievable, particularly if the man is over sixty."

Hitler, however, had other ideas. Vowing vengeance on Il Duce's betrayers and determined to reestablish Italian fascism, Hitler immediately began taking steps for Il Duce's rescue.

On July 27, just two days after Mussolini's arrest, Hitler appointed Otto Skorzeny, commander of a special commando unit, to find Il Duce and bring him to Germany.

It seemed an impossible job, but German agents were already so well established in Italy that they soon learned that Mussolini was being held on an island somewhere south of Rome. On August 18, from a small plane flying low over Ponza, Skorzeny had a glimpse of a man at the cottage window and guessed that it was Mussolini.

The appearance of the plane, however, caused a countermove by the Italians. On August 28, a Red Cross seaplane flew Mussolini from Ponza to Lake Bracciano, some twenty-five miles north of Rome. From there, an ambulance took him eastward for several miles up a twisting mountain road into the famous Gran Sasso skiing region of the Apennine mountains. Mussolini was held at an inn near the start of a cable railway that led to a mountain top resort.

During the week that followed, German planes made several low passes over the inn, and a German car was seen near the railroad station. On September 6, the guards took Mussolini up to the Campo Imperatore hotel on top of the mountain. The hotel had been cleared of summer guests. There, some seventy-five miles northeast of Rome, Mussolini spent the next six days in a roomy second-floor apartment.

On September 8, the new Italian government surrendered to the Allies. On September 11, the German army reacted by occupying Rome and capturing all officials of the Badoglio government who had been unable to flee. But Mussolini did not seem to be interested in the news. He listened to music on the radio, and played cards and chatted for hours with his guards.

Thanks to German agents, Skorzeny now knew exactly where Mussolini was being held. He flew over the mountain and picked out an open patch of ground near the hotel where his rescue team could land in gliders. He decided to split his force. While one group captured the railroad station at the bottom of the mountain, another would attack the hotel. Italy's surrender made it difficult to obtain cooperation from local police, but Skorzeny was ready to use force when necessary. He forced General Soleti of the Italian army to join the assault. Although he went unwillingly, Soleti did prevent bloodshed.

Early in the afternoon of September 12 the railroad station was captured without incident. A few minutes later, twelve gliders were released in the crisp air above the mountain. Each glider carried ten soldiers. Because the open patch of ground proved to be steeper than it appeared from the air, one glider crashed, seriously injuring its occupants. Three others, unable to land, veered off to safer ground in the valleys. But eight came down safely near the hotel.

General Soleti appeared first, calling for the guards not to shoot. Although the general was followed closely by a German officer who pressed a gun in his ribs, the Italian police did not open fire. Mussolini, watching from his second-floor window, also shouted for no shooting.

As it turned out, the police gave up easily. While some ran away others allowed themselves to be disarmed by the Germans.

It took just a few minutes for Skorzeny to reach Mussolini's room. For a moment, the German was not sure he had the right man. Mussolini looked old and ill. He was unshaven and a gray stubble covered his head.

Skorzeny explained the escape plan. Mussolini would be flown out in a light Storch airplane that had been landed with the gliders. At the airfield near Pratica di Mare, Il Duce would board a transport plane that would fly him to Munich, where he would be reunited with Rachele and his family, who had already been flown out of Italy. Humiliated at being rescued by the Germans, Mussolini was reluctant to agree to the plan, but Skorzeny insisted. Finally, at about 4:30 P.M., Il Duce emerged from the hotel in a shabby overcoat and dark, pork-pie hat. He did not smile, but he strode toward the plane with what one member of the hotel staff described as a youthful step.

Skorzeny, a big man, crowded into the plane with Il Duce. The German officer knew that the little Storch was dangerously overloaded, but he was not prepared to face Hitler alive if anything should happen to Il Duce. The plane, its engine straining, bounced over the rutted ground to the edge of the clearing, dipped its nose as if to plunge down the mountain, and then gradually steadied in controlled flight.

At midnight, still with Skorzeny, Mussolini arrived in Vienna in a Heinkel transport plane. After a much-needed sleep in a downtown hotel, he was flown to Munich where he was greeted by Rachele and his children. They were shocked by Mussolini's sickly color and shabby clothes. At a hotel, Rachele fussed over her husband. She discarded his old clothes, gave him a bath, and got him into a clean suit.

Next day, September 14, after a restful night, Mussolini flew to Hitler's headquarters in the Rastenburg forest for a meeting that lasted two days. Hitler had expected Mussolini to be eager for power and vengeance on those who had deposed him. But Il Duce did not seem to care. His indifference, however, did not change Hitler's plans. On the second day of the conference, the Fuehrer outlined what must be done.

Mussolini was to organized a new government, which would restore Italian fascism without the treacherous king. At first, his headquarters would be in Munich. Later, a spot for the new government would be found in northern Italy.

Although vengeance was foremost in Hitler's mind, he did not dwell on it at this time. Nor did the Fuehrer explain that Mussolini's new government would be little more than window dressing for the German occupation of Italy.

Hitler did, however, scold Mussolini for his defeatism.

"What is this sort of fascism that melts like snow before the sun?" the Fuehrer asked. Hitler said the war must be won, and as soon as victory came, Italy's rights would be restored.

By the second day of the conference, Mussolini was ready to do what Hitler asked. On the evening of September 15, under the direction of the Germans, Mussolini issued a radio communiqué to citizens of Rome saying that he had resumed supreme power of Fascist Italy. Next, he ordered the officials Badoglio had dismissed to resume their posts. He reconstituted the Fascist militia and ordered the party to support the German army. He absolved officers of the regular army and navy of their oath of loyalty to the king. Fascism from now on was to be free of royalty.

On September 17, Mussolini returned to Munich. Because the city was being bombed regularly, he was installed with his family in a castle safely removed from Allied targets. There, under the eye of German guards and with just one telephone line to link him to the outside world, he was to govern his new regime. Filippo Anfuso, Italy's ambassador to Germany, became Il Duce's telephone operator, receptionist, and secretary.

Anfuso, the only leading Fascist ambassador to remain loyal, was shocked at Mussolini's appearance. The man had shrunk. His neck was so thin that his collar hung like a noose. His eyes had sunk in their sockets. His unshaven chin made him look like a tramp. But what upset Anfuso the most was Mussolini's change in attitude. Il Duce was no longer a man of power.

Surprisingly, one of the first to visit Mussolini in the new Munich headquarters was Ciano. If it had not been for Edda's insistence, Mussolini probably would have refused to see his son-in-law. As it turned out, Ciano charmed Il Duce out of his anger and after two subsequent visits apparently convinced Mussolini he was not one of the conspirators.

Had he been aware of Mussolini's weak position, Ciano never would have entered Germany. Hitler was in full control, and Hitler had marked Ciano for revenge.

Mussolini received other loyal members of the party who agreed to support the new regime. Some of them helped plan new policies. In his discussions, Mussolini returned to some of the ideals of socialism that he had embraced in the early days of his career.

On September 18, in a radio message broadcast in Italy, he outlined the goals of the new regime. It would be a sort of republican socialism, a government without a king and other privileged upper-class "parasites." Based on an economy that supported the laboring class, it would, Mussolini said, be "going back to our origins."

Although the Germans liked the spirit of the speech, they were concerned about the Socialist ideas that Mussolini expressed.

In Rome, the speech was received with indifference. Even die-hard Fascists refused to accept posts in the new government. German agents in Rome advised Berlin to make the best of a bad situation. So the government was formed with mostly mediocre men whose only asset was loyalty to Il Duce.

Mussolini himself headed the Ministry of Foreign Affairs because no one else was willing to take the post. Fernando Mezzasomma, young and virtually unknown, was named to head the important Ministry of Propaganda. Other posts went to men who were either unknown or known by their bad reputation.

On September 23 all posts were filled, and three days later, the Germans flew Mussolini to Forli. With him was Rudolf Rahn, the German ambassador to the new government, who was to serve as Hitler's tireless watchdog for the next several months.

The first meeting of the new Cabinet was held at La Rocca, a villa near Forli, on September 27. In his opening remarks, Mussolini said that the war must continue and that the traitors who had overthrown fascism must be tried and punished by a special tribunal. After accepting these conditions, the cabinet agreed to call a general assembly to discuss other policies of the new regime and choose permanent headquarters for the new government. Mussolini wanted to return to Rome, but the Germans feared that they might not be able to keep him under control there. Also, there was fear that Rome might soon fall into Allied hands.

From the moment of his return to Italy, Mussolini was frustrated by his German masters. He could achieve nothing, he complained to Rahn, if Germany continued to interfere. After the cabinet meeting, he wrote to Hitler saying that German control in Italy should be limited to military affairs.

Hitler did not reply to the letter.

Mussolini meanwhile thought of reviving his old paper. If he could once again write for *Popolo d'Italia*, he might be able to rally the people once again to his dreams of destiny. But in the end he gave up the idea of returning to journalism. The thought of inevitable German censorship was more than his pride could stand.

On October 5, Rahn took him to Gargagno, a small village on the west shore of Lake Garda about one hundred miles from the German border. There, in a comfortable but remote villa, the Germans established the headquarters for the puppet government. Because there wasn't room to house other ministries, they were scattered around the countryside in various towns. Most were located in or near Salò, at the south end of the lake. The new regime became known as the Salò Republic.

It was to frustrate Mussolini through the remaining few months of his life.

21

Ciano

MUSSOLINI and his family moved into a small pink villa surrounded by vineyards. It had a magnificent view of Lake Garda, the largest lake in northern Italy, but lakes depressed him. He said they were dead, an unhappy compromise between rivers and seas. The dreary mists and rains of autumn also lowered his spirits.

The villa proved to be such a crowded and noisy household that the Germans soon provided another, nearby house, for Mussolini's office. In the domestic storms to come, he often used it as a retreat.

There was little to do but talk of the past with old Fascists. He sometimes spoke of the future but not the present. Mussolini could do nothing to stop the tragedy.

The Allies began landing in Italy on September 3. From the tenth to the fourteenth, a fierce defense near Salerno almost drove the invaders back into the sea, but the Allies brought more aircraft and heavy armor into the fight. Soon the long march north began. Foggia was captured on September 26. Naples fell on October 1.

The Badoglio government declared war on Germany.

Although divided between two governments, most of the people were united in their desire for peace and their hatred of Germany. The Germans did not try to make friends.

In northern Italy, they began rounding up all the men they could find for the labor camps in Germany. The provinces of Trieste, Bolzano, and other regions taken from Austria in World War I were occupied by the Germans as enemy territory. Italian soldiers caught in these so-called operational zones were sent to Germany as prisoners of war.

Bands of partisan soldiers, dedicated to liberating Italy, sprang up everywhere. Their loosely organized guerrilla attacks against the Germans hastened the end of the war.

Through Rahn, Mussolini protested repeatedly that the operational zones belonged to Italy and their property and their citizens must be respected. The protests were in vain. Germany went on expanding the zones until October 10, 1943, when the Fuehrer ordered that all of northern Italy be placed under German military rule.

Mussolini had a government with nothing to govern. It did not even have proper recognition. Although Axis nations such as Rumania and Japan had recognized the Salò regime, neutral nations had ignored it. Even Franco withheld Spain's recognition, saying coldly to Mussolini's ambassador that Il Duce would soon be dead. Franco was not famous for his gratitude.

Under the care of a German doctor, Il Duce's health had actually begun to improve. The stomach pains had stopped. He slept normally and ate normal meals. He regained some of the weight he had lost, and his yellow complexion gave way to hints of pink. Some of his old enthusiasm returned, and he set to work on a manifesto outlining the policies and goals of the new regime.

Although the manifesto would be presented to a Fascist party congress, Mussolini probably knew that it was an exercise in futility; but it gave him a chance to express some of his new, liberal ideas. Also, he thought it might have a unifying influence on his divided country.

First priority, the manifesto said, was to dissolve the monarchy and nominate a new government leader. This post would be filled by elections every five years. Although the Fascist party would continue to control political education, party membership would no longer be a condition of government employment or appointment.

Mussolini had some progressive notions. Property could be owned privately, but owners who failed to make use of their land could lose it to the government. He also envisioned a community of European nations dedicated to fighting capitalism, particularly British capitalism.

The party congress, when it met in nearby Verona on November 14, had little interest in the manifesto, and Mussolini, perhaps sensing the mood of the people, did not attend. It was rowdy. Speakers were constantly interrupted by demonstrations and hecklers. Some in the crowd shouted insults against Mussolini and Clara Petacci. Socialists demanded representation. Even Communists wanted a voice in the new regime.

The main interest, however, was vengeance. Grandi, Ciano, and the other "traitors" must be brought to trial. Actually, Salò ministers had already appointed a nine-man tribunal to try the dissidents.

After the congress adjourned, the Salò Republic concentrated on preparations for the trial. Vengeance, too, was the main thing, perhaps the only thing, Hitler wanted from the puppet government. The Fuehrer's hate focused on "that anti-German, Ciano."

Mussolini thought at first that a trial might help unify the Fascist party, but he was torn by emotional family arguments. Edda, of course, violently opposed a trial. In the party's present mood, she knew her husband would be convicted and executed. Mussolini's other children were also opposed. Only Rachele, who had never forgiven Ciano for his grand council vote against Il Duce, favored a trial.

Party secretary Alessandro Pavolini, who named the tribunal, was careful to pick nine extremists. Rahn reported gleefully to Hitler that the judges were fanatics of the old guard who "will offer the guarantee that particularly in Ciano's case the death sentence will be pronounced."

Ciano had become the main villain. Grandi had escaped to Spain, and most of the others who had voted with him were hiding. Only five had remained in Rome. They had been arrested and sent to Verona's Scalzi prison to await trial.

Ciano, meanwhile, remained in Munich. He was not aware of the mood of the new fascism. He had stoutly declared his loyalty to Il Duce. In fact, he thought he had regained his father-in-law's affection and would soon be given a post in the new government. He was waiting for Mussolini's call.

The call never came. Instead, on October 19, German agents put him on a plane and flew with him to Verona where he was promptly arrested and locked up in the Scalzi. He arrived with a mystery woman.

Felicitas Beetz, who described herself as an interpreter, accompanied Ciano on the flight and visited his prison cell frequently. Her real name, however, was Hildegard Berger. She was a secret agent assigned to get Ciano's diaries and papers.

The confidential documents, in which Ciano had given his candid views on everything from Hitler and the Nazis to Mussolini and all the other figures in his long regime, became the prize in a cat-and-mouse game that continued until the last day of Ciano's life.

Frau Beetz was secretly working for Heinrich Himmler who, as head of Nazi police, had become the second most powerful man in Germany. Himmler believed Ciano's papers would reveal information damaging to Ribbentrop, his chief rival in Germany's political jungle.

Only Edda knew where the papers were hidden, and she would produce them only if Ciano were freed.

He remained in the Scalzi, but repeated delay of the trial gave Frau Beetz ample time to negotiate. Neither Himmler nor Edda trusted each other, but about two weeks before the trial they agreed on a plan for Ciano's "escape."

Two German agents, posing as Fascists, were to break into Ciano's cell and take him to an airport where a plane would fly him to Hungary. After arriving there safely, Edda was to give Frau Beetz the papers. Apparently even Hitler, who wanted to keep the papers out of Allied hands, approved the escape plan. It was called Operation Count. It remained only a plan.

At the last minute, Himmler demanded that some of the papers be delivered before Ciano was freed. This demand was still being discussed when Hitler canceled Operation Count.

Two days later, on January 8, 1944, the trial began.

Ciano and five others faced a panel of stern, black-robed men. The trial chamber in Verona's Castelvecchio was jammed with loyal Fascists whose faces were equally stern. From the beginning, crowds outside the castle behaved like a lynch mob. Many threatened to kill the defendants if the judges failed to do the job.

Mussolini did not attend. Emotional pleas from Edda and the other children had exhausted him, and he knew that the evidence did not support charges of conspiracy. It was a sham, but for the sake of party unity, he believed it was necessary.

Mussolini also wanted to prove to Hitler that Italians could be just as tough and hardhearted as the Germans. The Fuehrer had repeatedly goaded Il Duce by predicting that the sentimental Italians would never go through with the trial. The goading sealed the fate of the defendants.

On trial with Ciano were Emilio de Bono, Carlo Pareschi, Tullio Cianetti, Luciano Gottardi, and Giovanni Marinelli. de Bono had been an army marshal. Pareschi had been minister of agriculture. All were found guilty of conspiracy.

Marinelli, who was deaf and had been sitting at the end of the table during the grand council meeting, may not have been aware which side he was voting for. He certainly had little understanding of the issues. But the court did not consider his deafness an excuse. Only Cianetti, the man who had written a letter to Mussolini the day after the council meeting, recanting his position, was spared. He was sentenced to thirty years in prison. The others were sentenced to death.

After the sentences were read, Marinelli had to ask Ciano, who was sitting next to him, what his fate was.

"Death, as for the rest of us," Ciano answered loudly.

Marinelli fainted in his chair.

When he recovered he was taken with the other defendants back to the Scalzi. There they all signed petitions to Mussolini asking for a reprieve.

MEANWHILE, in the remaining hours, Edda made a final, desperate attempt to save her husband. She wrote three letters, one to the commanding German general in Italy, another to Hitler, and the third to her father. To all, she threatened to turn the diaries and papers over to the Allies if Ciano were not delivered safely to Switzerland in three days.

For her own safety, Edda then fled to Switzerland where she waited in vain.

The Fascist extremists, meanwhile, not trusting Mussolini to reject the appeals for reprieve, refused to present them to him. Instead, they persuaded the senior military officer in Verona to reject them. The rejected appeals were then returned to the men in the Scalzi in the early hours of January 11 where the condemned men were already preparing for death.

The prison chaplain heard confessions and gave communion. At 9 A.M. the five condemned men were handcuffed and led into the prison courtyard. Marinelli, overcome with emotion, had to be supported by guards. Ciano cursed loudly until de Bono asked him to be quiet. A small crowd of prison guards and lawyers watched the men climb into a prison van.

The van took them to a shooting range at Forte San Procolo, a suburb of Verona. Five chairs had been lined up against a wall. The condemned were told to sit on the chairs backward so that their hands could be tied to the chair backs. Their own backs faced the firing squad, a militia unit of twenty-five men. A German firing squad stood ready nearby in case the Italian squad failed to obey orders.

Shrieking and moaning, Marinelli had to be roped to his chair. The other prisoners waited quietly, but at the last moment one voice shouted: "Long live Italy! Long live Il Duce!"

The first salvo of the small Italian rifles seemed to have little effect. One man remained erect in his chair as if he had not been hit. The other four lay twitching on the ground. Broken fire from the militia ended most of the agony. Then, after the cease-fire had been given, the squad commander and a few others approached and finished the victims off with pistols shots.

A German officer examined Ciano's body to make sure there had not been a last-minute substitute.

Reaction to the executions was immediate and strong. Although Fascist extremists cheered the death of the "traitors," the executions, instead of uniting the country, only gave further fuel to political strife. In Milan, the Salò government was generally condemned. In Rome, the five men were regarded as martyrs. Ciano was praised as a hero. Mussolini was pictured as a butcher with bloody hands.

Although outwardly calm during the trial and execution, Mussolini's inner turmoil left deep scars. Those who witnessed the executions were required to describe them to him again and again in every detail. He tried to justify the executions as a national necessity. But he really did not see Ciano's death that way. Like the death of Bruno, it was a family tragedy.

Hoping for a reconciliation with Edda, he began writing her long, plaintive letters. She gave short, cold replies. Reconciliation, she said, would never be possible. Never! Meanwhile, she arranged to give the papers to the Allies.

Shortly after the executions, a rumor of Mussolini's death raised cheers of joy in Rome. When told people were saying he was dead, Mussolini replied thoughtfully, "They may be right."

22

Retreat to Milan

ITALY WAS IN TORMENT.

The Germans, desperate for manpower, now used any excuse to send male Italians north as forced laborers. Antiaircraft batteries around many German cities were manned by Italians.

Even at home, Italians slaved for the Germans. When factory workers in one war plant decided to strike for better conditions, the Germans sent 20 percent of the men north. The strike fizzled, but resentment rose everywhere.

Partisan bands grew and became more organized. In some regions the partisans controlled the countryside completely. Fascists and Germans stayed clear of these districts; any militia or police that remained were pinned down in the cities like besieged troops.

News from the front remained bad. The Allies advanced steadily, threatening Rome and the industrial north.

Mussolini, with no military power, could not even control his own government. Rahn checked every detail of the Salò administration. Even appointment of minor city officials had to be approved by the German ambassador. Mussolini asked vainly for more authority. Without an army, the Salò Republic could not win independence from Germany. There were four Italian divisions being trained in Germany, but Hitler was reluctant to let them go home. He talked of using the men in munitions factories.

Disharmony among Salò officials added to Il Duce's frustration. It was almost impossible to get anything done.

Mussolini found some satisfaction in political theory. He dreamed of reviving his early socialism. His new government, he told friends, should offer improved justice, fairer distribution of wealth, and a stronger voice for labor. Over Rahn's strong protest, Mussolini decreed that Italy's major industries be socialized, with their management shared equally by labor and capital.

Fiat and some other large companies adopted the decree in order to ease worker unrest, but Rahn, seeing it as a step toward communism, would not help implement it. Many companies that tried to introduce the shared management plan found little enthusiasm among workers because the plan carried the stamp of fascism, and the workers now distrusted fascism in any form.

Eventually, his patience with Rahn gone, Mussolini demanded a talk with Hitler to discuss expansion of the Salò Republic's authority. The Fuehrer received him in Germany on April 22, 1944, and this time he let Mussolini open the meeting with a long speech. Il Duce asked that troops interred in Germany be returned to Italy, that German control over the Salò regime be eased, and that German military rule in the operational zones be at least partially lifted. Italian citizens, Mussolini stressed, must believe that the Salò Republic, not the Germans, ran the country. Only in this way, he said, could Italian morale, so necessary for the Axis cause, be restored.

Il Duce's speech took most of the morning, and Hitler, having afternoon appointments, postponed the session until the evening. He came armed with insults, saying that Germany, after placing great hope in the personality and ambitions of Mussolini, suddenly found that he and his regime had vanished overnight. Such a thing, Hitler declared with a knowing smirk for his aides, could never happen in Nazi Germany.

Italian soldiers, Hitler declared, were generally unreliable. Even as workers they did not match French laborers who had been imported to Germany. The interred Italian soldiers Il Duce wanted released were mostly Communists, Hitler said, not worthy of concern. The operational zones, Hitler added, had to be kept under firm control to prevent a partisan crisis behind the lines of combat.

Hitler concluded with expressions of goodwill but gave no promise of giving Mussolini more control over his government. Il Duce had achieved nothing.

For him, the best part of his trip came the following day when he reviewed and spoke to Italian troops under training in Germany. He promised the thirteen thousand officers and men of the San Marcos Division that they would soon return to their homeland where they could experience "the joy of opening fire on this medley of bastard races and mercenaries, who in invaded Italy respect nothing and no one."

For a moment, Mussolini sounded like his old self. Indeed, talking to the troops did lift his spirits, but back at Lake Garda more bad news greeted him.

Russia advanced steadily on the eastern front. The Allies advanced steadily in Italy. Rome fell on June 4. Two days later, a huge Allied fleet landed an army in Normandy on the Atlantic coast of France. Although the long-expected invasion of France was of top importance, for Mussolini the fall of Rome was the most devastating blow of the war.

He ordered three days of national mourning and issued a proclamation urging greater war effort. In a newspaper article he described his distress over the thought of black troops on the streets of Rome. The appeal to racial hate gave an indication of Mussolini's desperate spirits.

The partisan threat grew. Most partisans were led by Communists, a few by Socialists, but they were generally not motivated by political creeds. They wanted revenge. They wanted peace. They wanted a chance to rebuild Italy under a free and independent government.

Partisans in and around Milan became so strong that the police occasionally went into hiding. One night, a thousand partisans entered the city unopposed. The Germans fought back with reprisals. After a German truck was attacked by partisans, the Nazis executed fifteen political prisoners in Piazalle Loreto, a public square. Bodies were left where they fell, to be collected by grieving relatives. The outrage at Piazalle Loreto was remembered when it became the bloody arena for Mussolini's final appearance.

By the end of June 1944, the Salò Republic's "rule" was confined to the Po Valley. Other regions behind the lines were either under German "operational" grip or controlled by partisans. The situation was so desperate that Hitler finally agreed to send two of the German-trained divisions back to Italy to fight partisans. It was feared, however, that the men, who had been away for many months, might desert as soon as they reached Italy. Hitler invited Il Duce back to Germany to speak to the troops and strengthen their resolve before sending them into battle.

Mussolini left Lake Garda headquarters on a special train July 15. In addition to speaking to troops, he would also see Hitler again. On this, their last meeting, everything went wrong.

Just a few hours before they were to confer, Hitler was almost blown to oblivion. A bomb, planted by conspirators, shattered the Fuehrer's conference room. By some miracle, Hitler escaped harm, but he was still in a highly agitated state when he and his staff greeted Mussolini's train.

There was little communication. The Germans were interested only in rounding up and executing the conspirators. They had no patience with Italy's tiresome problems. Hitler was almost dreamy-eyed over the conviction that his escape was a miracle ordained by heaven. He explained to Il Duce that he had been spared in order to complete the great work still to be done.

Mussolini, secretly pleased that he was not the only one troubled by conspirators, congratulated Hitler on his escape and then tried to discuss current problems. Hitler was in no mood to listen, but he did agree to return all four, rather than just two, divisions to Italy. Nothing more was accomplished at the meeting, and as it turned out, just two divisions were actually returned.

Axis forces continued to retreat on all fronts. On August 15 the Allies landed on the southern coast of France and met little resistance. Paris was liberated on August 25. In Italy the Allies captured Florence and established a front line just 150 miles south of Lake Garda.

The Salò government would soon have to retreat. The question was where?

Most Fascists favored moving to a defensive position in the Alps, possibly north of Lake Como near the Swiss border. Preparations were being made for this move when the Allies halted just north of Bologna and dug in for the winter. The war stagnated.

A dreary succession of hopeless winter days descended on Lake Garda. For Mussolini the main diversion was domestic trouble touched off in October when Clara Petacci arrived and set up housekeeping in a nearby villa. Once imprisoned by the Badoglio government and later freed by the Germans, she had come to Lake Garda to be near her lover.

Rachele lost all patience. She went to the Petacci villa, confronted her rival, and demanded that she leave. Versions of the drama vary. Clara reportedly fainted, but not until after she had somehow made clear she would not leave. Rachele returned home in a rage and took poison. Both she and her rage, however, survived. Until the storm passed, Mussolini slept at his office where he dreamed of little plots to deceive the Germans.

EARLY IN DECEMBER, without consulting Rahn, Mussolini decided to make a public appearance in Milan. The Fascist radio there gave the first hint of it on December 15 by announcing that an unusual event would take place the following day. The event proved to be Mussolini speaking before a carefully selected Fascist audience in Milan's Lyric Theater. It was the last public speech of his career.

Mussolini described the betrayals that had caused the downfall of the old fascism and boasted of the strength and the promise of the new regime. He said the Allies were losing strength and the will to fight on. He said secret weapons held great promise for the Axis. And he concluded with an emotional call for unity and national sacrifice. Although the speech had no lack of bold statements, observers said it was not delivered with the intensity and conviction of Il Duce's earlier orations.

Mussolini made several public appearances during the remainder of his three-day stay in Milan. He never failed to prompt cheers from the crowds wherever he appeared. True, the crowds were carefully organized, but he still knew how to rouse Italian emotions.

He was pleased, but he had to return like a prisoner to his Lake Garda headquarters. There a friend welcomed him with kind words on his success in Milan. Mussolini gloomily replied, "What is life? Dust and altars, altars and dust."

He spoke frequently of death. He began to spend hours alone. There was little to do. He did make one change in his government, appointing Paolo Zerbino minister of the interior to replace Guido Buffarini-Guidi. Rahn suspected Zerbino of anti-German sentiments and protested. Mussolini shrugged.

Meanwhile, under strict secrecy, Rahn and a few other high-ranking Germans had opened negotiations for a separate treaty between the Allies and German forces in Italy. Such a treaty would abandon the Salò Republic to an uncertain destiny. But unknown to the Germans, Mussolini had also been negotiating peace. Ironically, both sides were working through Cardinal Ildefonso Schuster, a representative of the Vatican.

During this period visits from reporters gave Mussolini the chance to play the role of elder statesman and political prophet. To one journalist he predicted: "You will see that America will forget its old inferiority complex in relation to England, and then they will not this time return to isolation, as they did after the other war. They will pursue a world policy. . . ."

In a candid mood, he said, "I have never made a mistake when I followed my instinct, only when I obeyed reason. . . . I am finished. My star has set. . . . Perhaps I was destined only to point the way to my people. I should have rested content on a firm, secure basis. But have you ever known a prudent calculating dictator?"

And Mussolini was not quite ready to rest.

On March 26, Filippo Anfuso, his current ambassador to Germany, arrived with frightening news. The Allied armies were little more than sixty miles from Berlin on the western front, while the Russians were just forty or fifty miles away to the east. Almost all leading Nazis, Anfuso said, were resigned to Germany's defeat and were looking for ways to save their skins. It seemed that only Goebbels and Hitler himself were determined to continue fighting.

Mussolini told Anfuso about the secret negotiations with Cardinal Schuster, and for the next few weeks Anfuso and Mussolini feverishly explored possibilities for a separate peace. Their secret sessions became urgent on April 9 when the Allies, opening their spring offensive, advanced into the Po River valley. Anfuso urged Mussolini to move his government to Milan where he could seek peace free of German interference.

On April 14, without revealing his real reasons, Mussolini told Rahn of the plan to move. Milan, Mussolini said, would place the government closer to the defensive position in the mountains north of Lake Como. Rahn was suspicious. He persuaded Anfuso to return at once to Berlin, and he got Mussolini's reluctant promise to remain at Lake Garda.

Soon after Anfuso left, however, Mussolini broke the promise. On the evening of April 18, after trying to quiet Rahn's protests by saying the move was only temporary, Mussolini left Lake Garda. He and most other members of the Salò Republic traveled in a convoy of trucks and vehicles with a small German escort. He had no plans to return.

Government headquarters were soon established in the Milan prefecture, or city hall, a large building in the center of the city. There, Mussolini played out his last, frantic days as dictator.

23

Flight to Lake Como

THOSE IN THE SALÒ REGIME who survived recalled Mussolini's stay in Milan as a week of confusion and uncertainty. The nightmare of contrary orders, conflicting reports, and changing tides of emotion make it difficult to this day to agree on exactly what happened.

Among the various offices hastily set up in the prefecture, there were few men who understood the situation, and none with the imagination or the nerve to act. Even the man who once ruled Italy did not seem to know exactly what he wanted.

For a time it seemed that Mussolini was seeking a truce that would assure the safety of himself, his family, and those who had remained loyal to him. His pride, however, kept getting in his way. To some followers it was impossible to talk of giving up. When with them, Mussolini talked only of fighting on to the last man. When with others, he said the regime must not surrender to the Allies because that would simply be giving the government to Badoglio and the king. With still others, he spoke of making a truce with whatever organization gave the best terms.

It was probably sentiment that led him to seek a truce with the Socialists. The Milan Socialists, however, had long memories and refused to have anything to do with the man who had abandoned the party during its pre-World War I crisis.

Mussolini asked next for a meeting with representatives of

the Liberation Committee, a group representing most of the partisan factions in and around Milan. He still felt it necessary to hide truce negotiations from the Germans. Rahn and his staff, fortunately, had remained at Lake Garda, expecting Mussolini's early return.

The highest-ranking German at the Milan prefecture was Lieutenant Fritz Birzer, who cared nothing about negotiations. His job was to protect Mussolini. With the Italian front crumbling, and with the dreamy lack of reality at the prefecture, Birzer's job was growing more difficult by the minute.

Bologna fell on April 21. On the same day, Allies began crossing the Po River. Fascists caught in liberated districts were often shot outright by the partisans. On April 23, Parma fell to the Allies, and partisans captured Genoa. Fascist blood flowed.

Buffarini-Guidi urged Mussolini to flee to Switzerland. Il Duce, however, answered his former minister of the interior by saying fascism must make a last stand in the mountains. To Birzer this sounded like insanity, but when he asked for more details, Mussolini said he had not really decided what to do.

On the afternoon of April 23, Mussolini left the prefecture for a brief visit with Clara Petacci, who had followed the convoy to Milan. She and her brother had recently refused to fly to safety in Spain with their parents. Now, over Mussolini's protests, she vowed to share her destiny with his.

On returning from this operatic episode, Mussolini telephoned Rachele and told her to go at once to Monza, a city just north of Milan, and await instructions.

On April 24, Allied planes strafed the streets of Milan. Partisan strength in the city grew. In the midst of the confusion at the prefecture, Mussolini received a telegram from Hitler who was then under siege in his Berlin bunker. It was a strange message.

The struggle for existence or nonexistence has reached its climax. Using huge forces and materials, Bolshevism and Judaism have engaged themselves up to the hilt to assemble their destructive forces on German territory, to precipitate our continent into chaos. Nevertheless, with their obstinate scorn of death, the German people and all the others who are animated by the same sentiments will fling themselves to the rescue, however hard the struggle, and with their incomparable heroism will change the course of the war at this historic moment which will decide the fate of Europe for centuries to come.

The Fuehrer's suicide death was just six days away.

April 25 dawned in silence. The Milan prefecture no longer bustled with confusion. Overnight, many Fascists had abandoned Mussolini to go into hiding. The few loyal men who remained still could not agree on what to do.

Birzer, almost frantic over the uncertainty, stood outside Mussolini's office waiting for instructions. He had placed his small squad of soldiers on alert, ready for any development.

Mussolini finally decided, if negotiations failed, to retreat to the Alps. He called Rachele in Monza and instructed her to take the children to Villa Mantero, closer to Lake Como. He apparently hoped to meet her there on his way to the mountain stronghold. Meanwhile, he waited for word from the Liberation Committee.

By coincidence, the committee had chosen Cardinal Ildefonso Schuster as their negotiator, the same man who had earlier discussed secret peace feelers with both Rahn and Mussolini.

On the afternoon of April 25, the cardinal scheduled a meeting between partisan leaders and Mussolini at the Archbishop's Palace in Milan. He sent his car to the prefecture to pick up Il Duce and members of his staff. Birzer, who almost failed to see Mussolini and four other men leave, barely managed to find a seat in the old car. He had no idea where they were going. He only knew that he must stay close to Il Duce.

The Fascists arrived early, and Mussolini spent an uncomfortable hour with the cardinal in polite but idle conversation. When the partisan representatives did arrive it was obvious at once that they had expected to sit down in the conference room, not with Mussolini, but with the Germans.

Although the partisans were surprised, they were willing to talk. Mussolini, however, was almost speechless with anger. It was the first he had heard of a German bid for separate peace. Even though he had been willing to make a separate peace that would have left the Germans to fight the war alone, he did not believe the Germans had the right to "deceive" and "betray" him. Despite the cardinal's call for patience, Mussolini stomped out of the palace.

There would be no further talk of truce.

Back at the prefecture, still hot with anger, he ordered everyone to pack. Clothing and government files were thrown helter-skelter into boxes and suitcases. Mussolini put his secret papers and some large bundles of cash into a trunk. Meanwhile, several cars and trucks, hastily collected, lined up outside the prefecture.

The government officials, it was decided, would leave for the mountains at once. The Fascist militiamen who had volunteered to defend the mountain stronghold would leave a few hours later as soon as their leader, Alessandro Pavolini, could organize them and find suitable transportation.

Mussolini hastily wrote out a decree releasing soldiers of the regular army of their oath to the Salò Republic. The decree applied to few, but it eased Il Duce's conscience. Besides, he had grown weary of bloodshed.

He urged no one to retreat with him. And indeed, when men who had earlier resolved to fight to the finish quietly disappeared, Il Duce said nothing against them.

At 8 P.M. on April 25, led by Birzer and his troops, the

convoy pulled out of the courtyard of the prefecture and headed for Lake Como. Clara Petacci followed in a car driven by her brother, Marcello.

Mussolini reached the town of Como on the south end of the lake at 9 P.M. and decided to wait for Pavolini and his militiamen to join him the next day. But Como's chief of police warned Il Duce that the partisans were sure to make a lengthy stay dangerous. Mussolini decided to move on. First, however, he wrote a letter to Rachele, whom he had been unable to reach by phone.

> "Here I am, at the last stage of my life, at the last page of my book. We two may never meet again, and that is why I am writing and sending you this letter. I ask your forgiveness for all the harm I have unwittingly done you. But you know that you are the only woman whom I have ever really loved. I swear it before God, I swear it before our Bruno in this supreme moment. . . ."

He advised her to head for the Swiss border with the two youngest children and start a new life. If the Swiss should refuse her entry, he told her to surrender to the Allies.

> Take care of Anna and Romano, especially Anna who needs it so badly. You know how I love them. Bruno in heaven will help you. My dearest love to you and the children.

At 3 A.M., April 26, the convoy left Como. It stopped at Menaggio, a few miles up the west shore of the lake. Mussolini housed himself in a villa while the rest of his escort rested in an empty schoolhouse.

At dawn, a column of two hundred vehicles carrying the volunteer militiamen started north from Milan. The men had once sworn to defend Mussolini until death, but their loyalty had worn thin. Pavolini should never have left the men alone, but when he reached Como and learned that Mussolini had continued north, Pavolini went ahead by himself to get instructions. By the time he returned to Como, the partisans had scattered most of his army.

When he headed north again early on April 27, Pavolini drove one armored car containing a handful of men, all that remained of the militia.

Fortunately, about the time Pavolini arrived in Menaggio, a German antiaircraft detachment of about two hundred men in several trucks rumbled into town. The Germans, commanded by Lieutenant Fallmeyer, had been ordered to go north. Because their route led around Lake Como, Fallmeyer agreed to combine his force with Birzer's small escort. Together the two units made an impressive convoy.

Meanwhile, Elena Curti, another of Mussolini's former mistresses, had appeared at Menaggio. With the end drawing near, she also wanted to be at Il Duce's side. Clara Petacci glared at the new arrival, but before a fight could erupt, the Curti woman decided to return on her bicycle to Como in a vain effort to find the rest of Pavolini's troops.

Without the troops, the plan for a last stand in the mountains evaporated. Mussolini, however, refused to ask for asylum in Switzerland, and his resolve was strengthened by a report that Rachele and her two children had been turned back at the border. The Swiss would accept no more fugitives from fascism. Il Duce pressed on now simply because flight seemed better than stopping to wait for the end, and perhaps, with the help of the German soldiers, he could force his way through Switzerland to Germany.

The column left town before dawn on April 27. The vehicles labored up a narrow road that clung to the cliffs above the lake. First light revealed a faint but beautiful alpine scene. Most of the travelers, however, were too worried or frightened to appreciate the view.

Just after dawn at Musso, a small town overlooking the lake, shots broke the silence. The column lurched to a halt, stopped by a partisan roadblock. For a few tense seconds rifle shots and the rattle of machine-gun fire echoed across the lake. Then came silence. A white handkerchief was raised on a rifle barrel beyond the roadblock.

The partisans clearly had the advantage. The column could not advance, and retreat down the narrow mountain road would be almost impossible. Flight had ended.

24

Death

SOON AFTER the white handkerchief appeared behind the barricade, three partisans showed themselves cautiously. As Fallmeyer went forward slowly to negotiate, one of the partisans spoke to him in German.

Both sides quickly made clear that neither wanted a fight. Fallmeyer explained that his orders were to go north and eventually leave Italy. The partisans said they had been ordered to let no one pass, but their commander might make an exception. First, however, he must be brought from Dongo, the next town north, to talk to the Germans. Fallmeyer agreed to wait.

At the time, of course, the partisans had no idea that the convoy carried all that remained of the Fascist government in Italy.

Count Pier Luigi Bellini delle Stelle, code-named Pedro, a former law student, soon appeared to begin talking, through the same interpreter, with Fallmeyer.

Ever since news of Milan's fall had reached him the previous day, Bellini had been having unbelievable success in his district. Although his unit, the 52nd Garibaldi Brigade, numbered only twenty-five men, he had led the commander of the German garrison at Dongo to believe there were two hundred armed men in the hills.

The commander had surrendered to the "superior" force

without firing a shot. A few hours later, Bellini had worked the same trick on another German garrison to the north. Arms taken from the soldiers had been quickly distributed in the villages so that Bellini's force had indeed grown. Now he was ready to try a bluff on the German officer who led the convoy.

Bellini suggested that the officer come with him to Morbegno, a town fifteen miles up the road, where an agreement could be discussed in comfort. Fallmeyer agreed and the two men drove off in Bellini's old car. Meanwhile, following Bellini's earlier order, everyone who could hold a weapon—small boys, women, old men—had turned out to stand at the roadside, displaying one of the recently captured guns.

It made exactly the impression on Fallmeyer that Bellini had hoped. Even though Fallmeyer led two hundred well-trained men, he was convinced he could not win a fight with the partisans in Bellini's district.

Bellini did not hurry the conference. It was close to 2 P.M. when Fallmeyer returned to report that the partisans only wanted to prevent the escape of Fascists. The vehicles could continue if they stopped at Dongo, one mile up the road, for an inspection to make sure no Fascists were hidden in the trucks. Birzer protested, but Fallmeyer said they were hopelessly outnumbered. There was no other choice.

Poking his head inside the rear door of the armored car, Birzer explained the situation to Mussolini and urged him to put on a German helmet and German overcoat and ride with German soldiers in the back of one of the trucks. Il Duce reluctantly agreed.

Clara Petacci tried to enter the truck with her lover, but the Germans ordered her to return to her brother's car at the rear of the column. It seems that the Germans did not explain the situation fully to the other Italians. Most of them were rounded up by the partisans even before the column moved on to Dongo.

A suspicion, apparently aroused by the number of Fascist

officials taken at the roadblock, grew among the partisans that Mussolini might be in one of the trucks. Even if there had been no suspicion, it is unlikely that he would have escaped. Years of self-serving propaganda had made his face known to all Italians.

Soon after the column stopped in Dongo's town square, Mussolini was discovered and hauled out of his truck to stand blinking among elated partisans. His face showed immense weariness but no sign of fear.

The Germans, relieved of their unwanted passengers, drove off at once. Mussolini was taken to the municipal hall, joining the other partisan prisoners. Clara Petacci was among them, but at the moment, the partisans had not guessed her identity.

Mussolini's capture was reported immediately to the Liberation Committee in Milan. Partisan leaders there were surprised, elated, and not sure what to do. The committee's first instructions to Bellini were to treat Mussolini with courtesy and assure his safety. But the Communists, who dominated the Liberation Committee, secretly agreed that Mussolini and perhaps several others held at Dongo should be shot.

Walter Audisio, code-named Colonel Velario, was called on to carry out the assignment. Pretending that he intended to bring all the prisoners back alive for trial in Milan, Audisio left for Dongo at about dawn on April 28. He carried all the necessary passes to get through Allied and partisan roadblocks, and he was accompanied by a tough squad of partisans who were sure to follow his orders.

Bellini had no illusions. He was certain an attempt would be made to kill Mussolini. For this reason, he took Il Duce to a secret hideaway two miles outside of Dongo. Perhaps Mussolini would survive to face trial. Bellini thought it was important. Not only would the evidence of his crimes be instructive to the world, but a trial would also provide an important contrast to the regime Mussolini himself represented. The Fascists had never promoted humanity, civil rights, or justice in Italian law courts.

Mussolini did not remain long in his new prison before Bellini decided to move him again. At this point, however, Mussolini asked him to deliver a message to Clara Petacci in Dongo. The message was that she was to think of him no more.

Bellini was surprised. No one had yet guessed Clara's identity. But now Il Duce himself had given her away. Bellini immediately went to Dongo and talked at length to Clara. She persuaded him to let her join her lover.

Thus, when Mussolini was secretly moved again, two cars were needed. Clara rode in the first. In the second rode Mussolini disguised as a wounded partisan. He wore a head bandage that covered most of his face and he sat beside a female partisan who pretended to be a nurse. It was night and it rained hard.

They stopped often at partisan roadblocks. Bellini's plan was to take the two prisoners to a hideout on the other side of Como, but four miles north of the town they heard gunfire and learned that a few Fascist diehards were trying to defend the town against the advancing Allies.

Believing it was too risky to continue, Bellini decided to turn back to the town of Azanno. There, in the neighborhood of nearby Mezzegra, was a farmer who had always been willing to shelter partisans. He was sure to take in the prisoners.

It was pouring hard when they reached Azanno and left the cars. They climbed in the dark up a steep, rocky path to the farmer's cottage. Clara wore high-heeled shoes and had to be helped most of the way. She and Mussolini, who were both close to exhaustion, staggered to the cottage door. The farmer let them in the moment he saw Bellini.

Mussolini and Petacci were put in a room with a large double bed where they at once fell asleep. The time was 3 A.M., April 28, just a few hours before Walter Audisio was to leave Milan and begin his deadly search.

Despite his official passes, traveling proved difficult for the partisan colonel. At Como, local partisans, who did not want Mussolini taken out of their district, tried to stop him, but Bellini threatened to kill anyone who stood in his way. Finally, he was allowed to continue on the road to Dongo, but several other roadblocks delayed him. He did not reach his destination until 2 P.M.

There he had to face Bellini, who refused for a long time to say where he had hidden Mussolini. Bellini said it was his responsibility to deliver Il Duce and the other prisoners safely to the Liberation Committee in Milan.

"There is no question of that," Audisio shouted impatiently. "I have come to shoot them!"

More shouts, more heated words followed. Eventually, Audisio convinced Bellini that the Liberation Committee, despite orders to the contrary, secretly wanted the prisoners shot. Audisio had simply come to carry out the committee's orders.

Finally, with great reluctance, Bellini handed Audisio a list of his prisoners. Audisio immediately began making arbitrary marks on the list. He explained that in addition to Mussolini and Petacci, fifteen others must die. Some of those Audisio marked for death had been taken to an army barracks a few miles out of town. Bellini agreed to get them while Audisio and two partisan gunmen went to get Mussolini and Petacci from the farmhouse.

Bellini hoped this might delay Audisio long enough for the Allies to reached Mezzegra and rescue Mussolini, but it proved a vain hope. At about 4 P.M., Audisio reached the farmhouse and went immediately into the bedroom, shouting that he had come to rescue Il Duce and Petacci. Believing for a moment that Audisio was a fellow Fascist, Mussolini and Petacci hurried out to Audisio's waiting car.

The curving road descended toward Mezzegra, but the car had traveled only a few hundred feet when Audisio told the driver to stop. He ordered Mussolini and Petacci to get out.

Mussolini stumbled from the car. Petacci followed. Audisio pointed his machine gun toward the gateway to a private villa.

"Over there," he snapped.

After the two backed up against a stone wall, Audisio began shouting. He quickly listed many charges against Mussolini and then yelled that the Italian people demanded justice—now.

Realizing they had been fooled and that Audisio was pronouncing a death sentence, the two huddled together. Petacci clung to Mussolini's arm and faced Audisio, screaming. "No! You can't. You can't do that!"

"Get away from him," Audisio ordered. "Get away or you'll die, too."

Petacci did not move. Audisio pulled the trigger.

Click! Click!

The gun would not fire.

Petacci lunged forward, trying to grab the muzzle. Audisio jumped back and called for another gun. One of his men threw him his machine gun.

At this point, Mussolini, who had been silent, pulled open his jacket and said, "Shoot me in the chest." These were his last words.

The gun exploded to life in Audisio's hands, spewing death. Petacci fell first. Then Mussolini, with several bullets in his body, slumped on top of her. As the smoke cleared, Audisio ordered two of his men to guard the bodies. Then he jumped in the car and sped back to Dongo.

Audisio was in a frenzy. While Bellini and the mayor of Dongo protested, he ordered the fifteen prisoners whose names he had marked on the list into the town square. He lined them up and told them they had three minutes to say their prayers. Then he had his men open fire.

Marcello Petacci, Clara's brother, whose identity had finally become known, believing he, too, was to be shot, ran for the lake. He did not get far, however, before partisan bullets brought him down. His riddled body floated in the bloodied water just a few feet from shore.

On the morning of April 29, all the bodies, including Mussolini's and Petacci's, were loaded in a moving van and taken to Milan to be dumped in Piazalle Loreto, the square where the Nazis had earlier executed fifteen hostages. Mussolini, Petacci, and four others were hung by their heels from the girder of an abandoned gas station.

All through the day, in a raw display of hatred, men and women jeered and spat on the mutilated bodies. The square became so crowded at one point that it was hard to move. Late in the day, a pistol was fired into the body of Il Duce. The shot frightened many from the scene. In the evening, with the square almost empty, Allied soldiers removed the bodies.

Rachele heard of her husband's death on a radio newscast. The account of Mussolini's last moments at the side of his mistress was a personal torture to her. She surrendered in tears to the partisans in Como, but after a few days in jail, she was released to her family and her memories.

Today, Mussolini's body lies in the family cemetery at Predappio under a tombstone bearing the *fasces* emblem. Rachele Mussolini has reserved a plot for her grave beside his.

BIBLIOGRAPHY

Albrecht-Carrié, René. *Italy from Napoleon to Mussolini.* New York: Columbia University Press, 1960.

Bolitho, William. *Italy under Mussolini.* New York: Macmillan, 1926.

Churchill, Winston Spenser. *The Second World War, Vols. I–III.* London: Cassell, 1948–50.

Ciano, Galeazzo. *The Ciano Diaries, 1939–43* (Hugh Gibson, ed.). New York: Doubleday, 1946

Collier, Richard. *Duce! A Biography of Benito Mussolini.* New York: Viking Press, 1971.

Dolan, Edward F., Jr. *Adolf Hitler, A Portrait in Tyrany.* New York: Dodd, Mead, and Company, 1981.

Eisenhower, Gen. Dwight D. *Crusade in Europe.* New York: Doubleday, 1948.

Fermi, Laura. *Mussolini,* Chicago: University of Chicago Press, 1961.

Gregor, A. James. *Young Mussolini and the Intellectual Origins of Fascism.* Berkeley: University of California Press, 1979.

Halprin, William S. *Mussolini and Italian Fascism.* Princeton, N.J.: D. Van Nostrand Company, 1964.

Kirkpatrick, Sir Ivone. *Mussolini, A Study in Power.* New York: Hawthorne Books, 1964.

Machiavelli, Nicolò. *The Prince and the Discourses.* (Luigi Ricci and C. E. Metmold, tr.), New York: Random House, 1940.

Mack Smith, Denis. *Mussolini, A Biography.* New York: Vintage Books, 1982.

————. *Italy.* Ann Arbor: University of Michigan Press, 1960.

Mussolini, Benito. *The Cardinal's Mistress.* (Hiram Motherwell, tr.) New York: Bonibooks, 1930.

Mussolini, Rachele (with Anita Pensotti). *My Life with Mussolini.* London: Hale, 1956.

Shirer, William. *The Rise and Fall of the Third Reich.* New York: Simon & Schuster, 1959.

Skorzeny, Otto. *Secret Missions* (Jacques le Clerq, tr.). New York: E. P. Dutton, 1950.

Tompkins, Peter. *Italy Betrayed.* New York: Simon & Schuster, 1966.

Whittle, Peter. *One Afternoon at Mezzegra, The Story of Mussolini's Death.* Englewood Cliffs, N. J.: Prentice-Hall, 1969.

INDEX

208